Altadena Poetry Review
Anthology 2017

Editors

Elline Lipkin
Pauli Dutton

Altadena
Library
District

Published by Altadena Library District
600 East Mariposa Street
Altadena, CA 91001
www.altadenalibrary.org

Grateful acknowledgment is made to authors herein for permission to reprint their poems previously published elsewhere. Credit for prior publication is provided following each poem thus published herein. Each poet published in this anthology retains the copyright to his/her individual poem(s) published in this anthology.

The opinions expressed in this manuscript are solely the opinions of the poets published herein and do not represent the opinions or thoughts of the editors or publisher.

Library of Congress Cataloging-in-Publication Data

Altadena Poetry Review: Anthology 2017; edited by Elline Lipkin & Pauli Dutton.
  --1st ed.

150 p. cm.

ISBN 978-0692866146

1. Poetry—Authorship. 2. Southern California 3. Altadena, Calif. 4. Award-winning poets. 1. Elline Lipkin & Pauli Dutton.

17 18 19 10 9 8 7 6 5 4 3 2 1

First Edition: April 2017

Cover photo of a painting by George Gardner Symons: "Millard Canyon at Granite Gate." 1896.
    Donated to Altadena Library by Mr. and Mrs. Guy Fisher. Used with permission from the
    Altadena Historical Society.
Book design by Thelma T. Reyna
Cover design by Thelma T. Reyna and Dominic Gilormini
Printed in the United States of America

For the first time in the 15-year history of an Altadena poetry anthology, the creation of this book was led by co-editors: Elline Lipkin, Poet Laureate of the Altadena Library District; and Pauli Dutton, editor of the *Poetry & Cookies Anthology*, from which the *Altadena Poetry Review* evolved in 2015. The co-editors worked closely with a peer review panel of published poets and editors who discussed all submitted poems and selected the poems for inclusion in this book. The Anthology Selection Committee, all volunteers, was integral to this anthology.

ANTHOLOGY SELECTION COMMITTEE

For the third year in a row, the following poets participated as committee members in choosing poems for publication in the *Altadena Poetry Review: Anthology*, from 2015-2017. (New to the formal committee this year is Thelma T. Reyna, previous Poet Laureate and anthology editor.)

Tim Callahan

Gloriana Casey

Pauli Dutton

Gerda Govine Ituarte

Briony James

Thelma T. Reyna

Elsa M. J. Seifert

FOREWORD

"It is difficult / to get the news from poems," wrote William Carlos Williams in 1962, "yet men die every day / for lack / of what is found there." This excerpt from his poem "Asphodel, That Greeny Flower," then served as an epigraph and as part of the title of Adrienne Rich's book *What is Found There: Notebooks on Poetry and Politics,* published in 1994. Over 20 years later, the need for poets to convey the news — whether political, personal, or however embedded within the context of their worlds — speaks to the ongoing need for poetry that wants to be read and heard.

This anthology represents a wide range of poets writing across a spectrum of experience. Some are new to poetry, some have published many books; some have practiced their craft for years, some are just starting to find their way. Yet, all are called to this art, and all are eager to be heard. Honoring these voices and giving attention to the news found within these pages — epiphanies of personal experience, insights filtered through memory, commentary about contemporary times, and the pure whimsy and delight that comes from playing with words — is as important as ever.

While the poets included are of different generations, varied professional backgrounds, and divergent roots, all now reside within the greater Los Angeles area, and most live within the San Gabriel Valley. The pursuit of poetry is what brings them together in this book, alongside a love of seeking the right expression, the phrase that best captures the sense that what they have to say has importance.

I want to thank the Altadena Library District for its ongoing support both of this anthology and of the public programming I have been glad to organize, in addition to hosting the annual Poetry & Cookies reading event, with special acknowledgement of Mindy Kittay and her wonderfully supportive staff. This past fall, the library helped to sponsor the reading, "Poetry: The People's Art with Victoria Chang and Blas Falconer," and this spring, sponsored a poetry workshop with Suzanne Lummis that brought over 70 people pouring into the community room, all eager to spend time learning and writing. Many thanks, as well, to *Poets & Writers* for a generous grant which helped to sponsor this workshop through grants it has received from The James Irvine Foundation and the Hearst Foundations.

This anthology would simply not exist if not for the tireless efforts of Pauli Dutton, who, even in her retirement, continues to serve as a beacon for literary community in Altadena. Her persistence and her vision are the reason this book came into fruition and I cannot thank her enough for her guidance, dedication and sheer hard work. As well, the members of the Anthology Selection Committee put in many hours engaged in sensitive consideration and thoughtful debate about the work found within these pages. Their good spirit and serious work are another reason why this book is now out in the world. A final thank you to Thelma T. Reyna, who has continued to actively serve our literary community and whose expertise and generous hard work have been invaluable.

Thank you for taking the time to celebrate this exciting range of new work and new voices.

--Elline Lipkin, Ph.D.
Poet Laureate of Altadena 2016-2018

ACKNOWLEDGMENTS

Founded in 2003, the purpose of the original *Poetry and Cookies Anthology* and reading event was to provide new poets from Altadena and the surrounding communities an opportunity to have their work published and to read their poetry in public. The first *Poetry and Cookies* publication included work by 12 poets and grew to be over 50 poets by the time I retired in 2015. At that time, Thelma T. Reyna, the library's Poet Laureate 2014-2016 and a professional editor and publisher, led, at my request, the project and kept the tradition alive under a new name: the *Altadena Poetry Review: Anthology*. This title, signifying increased status and professionalism, offered the chance, in 2015 and again in 2016, to reach out to even more well-regarded San Gabriel Valley poets for publication consideration.

We have many to thank for this 2017 edition of the *Altadena Poetry Review: Anthology*. First is Elline Lipkin, Poet Laureate for the Altadena Library 2016-2018, who took on the huge task of spearheading this year's publication. Second is Thelma T. Reyna, who served this year as both a member and a guiding light to the APR Selection Committee. The seven other volunteer poets on the committee who worked closely with Elline Lipkin to help choose the poems are Tim Callahan, Gloriana Casey, Gerda Govine Ituarte, Briony James, Elsa Seifert, and myself.

From the beginning, the Friends of the Altadena Library has provided seed money to publish the anthology and to supply cookies and encouragement at the annual public reading event at which the anthology's published poets read their work. This year is no exception as the Friends helped fund two wonderful poetry programs organized by Elline: "Poetry: The People's Art" with featured poets Victoria Chang and Blas Falconer; plus a writing workshop led by Suzanne Lummis. Nevertheless, there have been more expenses that needed to be handled. For the past two years, Thelma and her publishing company, Golden Foothills Press, bore all the costs of publication, graphic design, printed materials, refreshments, and awards. After her time as Laureate ended, both Elline and I took on some of these expenses. As the costs of this year's publication loomed, Library Director Mindy Kittay encouraged Elline to ask the Friends of the Library for help. The organization enthusiastically replied in the form of a substantial donation. In response, Mindy wrote these encouraging words: "This program is much beloved by the community and another example of how libraries change lives by providing the tools, access and experiences that help each and every one of us reach our full potential."

For all of this, we would like to express our gratitude for the support, both personal and financial, of Altadena Library Director, Mindy Kittay, and the Friends of the Altadena Library. Without their assistance, this year's project would not have been able to continue. They well live up to the quote noted on the Friends of the Library homepage: "The word 'Friend' immediately brings to mind the people who help celebrate all the goodness in life and stand steadfast when times are troubled, who offer support when it's needed and offer counsel to help us see the straight path. We count on our friends and they count on us."

--Pauli Dutton

- Founder of *Poetry and Cookies (P&C) Anthology*
- Founder of P&C Public Reading Event
- Altadena Public Library: Principal Librarian, 1985-2014
- Friends of the Library Liaison
- Poet

TABLE OF CONTENTS

14

Alicia Elkort
She Runs to the Edge of Time in Pink Stilettos, *73*
Savior, *74*
Galaxies, *75*

Lowam Eyasu
Ode to My Mother, *76*

Lynn Fayne
Poetic Confusion, *77*

Emily Fernandez
Pile of Feathers, *78*

Mark A. Fisher
California Angel, *80*

R. Ford
The Sky Was in the Earth, *82*

G T Foster
Cien Años Family Site, *83*

Elsa Frausto
Moon Poem 1, *84*
Moon Poem 2, *84*

Martina Robles Gallegos
The Thorns of the Journey, *85*

Damian Gonzalez
October Eleventh, *86*

Charles Harmon
The Joy of Cooking, *87*

Hazel Clayton Harrison
Lover, *89*

David Humphreys, Jr.
A Kind of Yearning, *90*

20

LA GAVIOTA

The seagull knows no borders.
Flies on crisp ocean currents from
Oceanside to Tijuana.
No check points or toll roads.
No Green Cards, or citizenship papers required.

The winged creature roams freely
over Camp Pendleton Marine Base.
Squalls its call. An omen
to young Mexicans at the
other side of the border.

A bright future for Tijuana's son.
Superior in math and science,
head of the bugle corps, earning
the Netzahualcoyotl Award for Poetry.
Joel is signed up.

U.S. military recruiters,
a bonus for each recruit.
Mexican signs on the dotted line.
He pays a penalty for leaving home.
The seagull pays no fare.

U.S. citizenship, world travel,
a college education,
are broken promises.
A letter from Tio Sam
Joel returns home in a wooden box,
a downed sea gull.

--Vibiana Aparicio-Chamberlin

IT WAS AS IF YOU CAST A SPELL OVER ME

unable to move forward
        like a stump in the middle
        of a hayfield
arms loose
        hanging like paper chasers
        on clotheslines
senses blinded and overcast

but your magic
        didn't reach my insides
heart pumped a thousand times
        causing blood to circulate
        like a newfound waterfall
cutting through the Grand Canyon

--Maria A. Arana

THERE'S A SUITCASE IN THE CLOSET

There's a Suitcase in the Closet
So far it's gone unused
It's been there such a long time
In fact it's still brand new
It's waiting for a traveler
To take it by the hand
And go on some adventure
To some exotic land

There's a Suitcase in the Closet
A handsome price was paid
The price tag still attached to it
But still it's on display
It'd make a good companion
It'd make a fine valet
For one who seeks adventure
And looking for escape

Now is not the time
Someday when I'm fit
When I've got the money
Then I'll make the trip
Someday when the future
Becomes a bit more clear
Then I'll take myself
Far away from here

There's a Suitcase in the Closet
With wings it would take flight
And leave me here inside these walls
To mark the days and nights
I see it in the closet
It's looking back at me
It seems to be saying
Let's make some memories

There's a Suitcase in the Closet
I put it up for sale
At this time there are no takers
So it's to no avail
But now I'm having second thoughts
Of selling it at all
So I'm brushing off my passport
I'll use it after all

--Richard Ash

MOVING GROUND

It was the time when the salamanders
appeared underfoot, fresh from their primeval
lair, their nude red-brown forms lumbering
into the brush with a backward glance.

My small son saw the ground move,
dove to catch one – a prize in his palm.
He stared and stroked the gelatinous shape,
awaiting a message from dinosaur time
while hiking his first whineless mile.

I miss that boy who stooped to inspect
every worm and lizard in his path.
Does he still pick them up, amazed
at his luck, barely daring to breathe?

He lurches into the thicket of his twenties
without a backward glance.

--Susan Auerbach

TENDING

If you raise 'em from chicks,
they'll think you're their mother.

So we go to get four-day-old handfuls of fluff
at Wes's Feed Shack and the questions rush in:
Box or cage? Mash or scraps? We hover and dote--
Too hot, too cold? Will they eat their turds?
We coo so they'll know us; they stand still, learning.

>And just when the lamp is finally set for 90,
>they need 80; and just when
>we can contain their weightless squirming in our hands,
>they push back with sturdy feet,
>tails protrude, then two fans of mottled feathers
>edging out the baby fuzz.
>One day they stretch and shake untested wings
>and start to preen; the next, they fly leapfrogging
>back and forth in righteous flurry.

How to keep pace with the young's relentless flux?
Breast or bottle? Crib or bed? What, no nap?

This tending takes attending to the constancy
of change, to accumulating questions,
never ready for the next flex of the wings
as we stand still learning.

--Susan Auerbach

PUT YOUR MASK ON FIRST

Busy caregiver
Children
Almost grown up
Almost fully capable to handle
Life on their own

Caregiving continues
Occupied by disabled spouse
Impairment requires assistance
Demands of the day
Speed the hours away

Before helping others
Forgot to put my mask on first

Personal time gone
Personal health falters

Falling
A nosedive to crashing

Before helping others
Forgot to put my mask on first

Perishing in the flames of this lifetime

--Beth Baird

TALKING WALLS

The walls are talking
Hear them!
Rough- hewn timbers
Chopped by axes
A 15th century building concept

4 hundred years of occupation
Our family sentenced
To tragedy…to joy
To birth…to death
And continent… se….pa… ra…tion

A circular movement of spirits
Inhabiting these walls
Transcending the stories
Of a tiny farming community
Simultaneously echoing the history
Of the world from 1623 to the present

I hear the discussions
Current events discussed at **this** table
From Waterloo to Watergate
From burning witches to burning CDs
From German Occupation to 21st century refugees

The walls are talking

--Beth Baird

SAN GABRIEL MOUNTAINS

You are
the
Mountains
that welcome
me home.
My North,
my Compass,
my Guide
to all that is important.
At your feet I always find my way,
for you give direction.
In the light of day, eyes turn upward.
Your beauty astounds.
Purple, green, gray, golden, pink
colors that keep rhythm with the sun and clouds.
In the darkest night, you are still there blue upon blue.
You embrace all as life radiates from your peaks and canyons.
From every angle I see in new dimension, whispers of wisdom
for you always beckon to come and explore.
We shall never fully know you
though you are a constant.
You will stand with us through all time.

--Kathee Hennigan Bautista

HEADS UP

The sky winks down at an unsuspecting
suburban neighborhood
upper middle tract homes
south western style paint
redundant uniform shrubbery
the visitors
take notes, send messages,
think about which experiment
they want to try first
soccer Mom pulls the minivan into
the crystalline cement driveway,
is unaware of the medium, blue light
which beams down from the grey metal disk
three small odd shaped bodies come out
drop down
hold her in her paralysis
then take her up
fortunately, she will be back in time to get the kids
after practice
and not remember
a thing.

--Jack G. Bowman

MEMORY LAPSE

I was arrested on a serious charge.
But I'm not complaining, cause I'm living large.
Got my own room, got my own bed.
And a cook making sure every day that I'm fed.

When I exercise, I've got a great big yard.
And if there's trouble, I've got my own bodyguard.
I can read the newspaper, I can watch TV,
and I've got lovely ladies sending money to me!

The judge said I'll be here for the rest of my life.
I don't see my kids and I don't see my wife.
The things I miss most are my beer and my wine.
But every day I still try to have a good time.

Since the plans for my future are already laid,
life gave me "lemons," I'll make lemonade.
Can't let'em see me cry, can't let'em see me sweat.
And there are some things I hope God will let me forget.

My folks won't come to see me they all put me down.
They call me a "black sheep," they call me a "clown,"
If they send me anything it would be a big bomb.
I really can't remember, but they claim I killed Mom!

--Norma Burks

SOUL CATCHER

Caught by the sway of her body dancing
he could neither move nor speak.
And as she danced her finger cymbals
ensnared the rhythm of his heart.

Round and round him went her dance.
Round about him like a web
the sable length of her heavy hair
enfolded and entwined him.

And into her eyes, those dark pools,
his soul fell, was captured and held,
forever lost, forever trapped in
her body's swaying rhythms.

And once her sinuous dance was done
and the coins in her heavy low-slung belt
ceased their jingling and the long panels of
cloth fell furled between her naked thighs
none noticed that he was missing.

Then once more the music started with the *zurna's*
hornet whine, as the *oud's* strings were set
humming and hands rapid on the skin of the
dombek struck an insistent staccato beat.

Then again the coins in her belt were jingling
as to the beat her body was swaying. Then
her eyes full of darkness were searching.
She was on the hunt again.

--Tim Callahan

I SEE A GARDEN

I see a garden here, surrounding this patio.
Yes, I know you don't see even a patio, only
a patch of bare gray dirt bounded by bricks
and cinder blocks, with but a few paving stones,
soft-laid, in place. And, yes, that raised area
bounding it only holds piled up earth.

Yet, feel that earth! Let its moist wealth,
composted, slide through your fingers.
See? There are pill bugs scurrying,
trying to burrow into that sweetness
we've disrupted. Let them escape into it.
Isn't this soil sensual, to a mere touch?
Isn't the scent of the earth in your nostrils?
Isn't its richness a joy to behold?

Now, in that corner, tucked next to
the stucco wall, let your eyes wander
over the broad, dark green leaves of
the *Acanthus*. They are glossy and
many-lobed, delighting in the shade.
Yes, I know I haven't planted it yet.
That's a mere technicality.

I see myself in the coming summer
sitting on that patio in that shaded garden
with my feet up, drinking a cold beer as
I watch anise swallowtails mate in the fennel
so tall, with feathery light green leaves.
I see them fluttering over the blossoms
of the asters I will plant nearby. They
have blue petals and yellow centers.
They are not there. I see them clearly.

37

If I had not seen so many things
before they were, even the gardens
I've already planted wouldn't be.
A short while ago, as I surveyed
the top of this page, I saw myself
writing this poem.

--Tim Callahan

ASPEN LEAVES
(A PANTOUM) *

When aspen leaves are caught in a breeze
they're turned and spun, now green, now white
as gentle winds blow through the trees
and make them shimmer, dark and light.

They're turned and spun, now green, now white
as winds cause their white trunks to sway
and make them shimmer, dark and light
as fluttering leaves make shadows play.

As winds cause their white trunks to sway
the whole stand whispers a breathy song
as fluttering leaves make shadows play
and the trees sigh soft and long.

The whole stand whispers a breathy song
as gentle winds blow through the trees
and the trees sigh soft and long
when aspen leaves are caught in a breeze.

--Tim Callahan

---

* In a *pantoum*, made up of a series of (usually) rhymed quatrains, the second
and fourth lines of the preceding stanza are repeated as the first and third lines
of the next stanza. This goes on until the last stanza, when the third line of the
first stanza is repeated as the second line and the first line of the poem is repeated
in its last line.

ALHAMBRA RACCOON

Three in the morning
Outside my window
Sitting in the well-lit
Medical office parking lot
On the aisle surrounded
By painted spaces
Something too big to be
A cat grooming her fur
Very thoroughly licking
Glancing over calmly
At no imminent threat
Sauntering on to the east

Did she come from
The nearby rainflow channel?
What is this animal
Walking to find: dumpsters,
Trash bins, sidewalk
And lawn throwaways?
Maybe an abandoned pet?
Is her family closeby,
Or is this a solo traveler,
Long lost from mountains?
Well, it's one healthy body
With a beautiful black mask

Must enjoy the bounty
Of city life at night
Padding on asphalt
Avoiding white lines
How many more days
Will this creature forage?
Hopefully meets no car
Don't want to see
Roadkill on my way

To work away my hours
On this planet of the living
And the dead disposed

--Don Kingfisher Campbell

THREE-LAYER BROWNIE

Via biting wind and salivic surf, he eats through, purchased from a petite waterfall-haired cheerful teenage student, a chocolate mesa, to create a crumbly cliff revealing baked layering of a heated past. The recently refrigerated saran-wrapped surface of crusty dark brown plated mantle, held up by the deeper darker nearly black oreonic cream-filled muddy subsoil, in turn supported by an array of larger melted chips like gigantic boulders buried in a blonde cake base, methodically vanishes. All washed down an over half-century old teaching throat in waves of bubbly cranberry red water encased in lightweight recyclable aluminum from the virtually empty great dispensing machine monolith in the busy teacher's cafeteria rectangle on a planet blithely rotating finitely to a finish.

--Don Kingfisher Campbell

A LITTLE BIRD TOLD ME

Sad Daphne's life was such a mess.
She'd flunked another vocab test.

"This work is dumb! it hurts my head."
These stupid Latin words are dead."

"Oh yeah, " said magpie on the sill.
"I'll make it brief." He snapped his bill.

In shock, poor Daphne gave a shriek!
"I'm mortified! That bird did speak!"

 "Well MORT's another Latin base.
It speaks of death. I rest my case."

"But you're a bird. You've got no cred!"
"CRED is belief, just what you said!"

 "This is good fortune!" Daphne cried!
"FORT means good luck," the magpie sighed.

"Congratulations," then he spoke,
 "GRAT---it means thanks. You've got some hope!"

 "There is a science to word's name.
SCI means to know----so play the game!"

Roots are vital---so get them right!
VIT comes from Latin--it means life!"

"What is your name?" she asked of bird.
"My name is VOC, from voice you've heard."

So Daphne looked in words for roots.
Then VOC he cawed, "You've got it, Toots!"

"I've played the game and raised my score!"
"Yeah,"quoth the magpie. "Evermore!"

--Gloriana Casey

THE SUN KING

NO! Not Louis nor Versailles----but this one----
THIS Sun King, in the here and now on a
winter's day in the city of L.A.
While the corporate Armanis and Guccis
swarm the towers of grand capital gods,
here among the shadows, he stakes his rule.

In a kiosk throne he reigns, wrapped not in
ermine, but in flannel and dust. Proud he
sits as the Walt Whitman in Everyman.

Eyes closed--head back-- a Mona Lisa smile----
his face bathed in the early morning light.
For that moment, He is me ---I am him.
The universe bends now to reveal the
perfect day! For Ozymandias fades,
and THIS Sun King warms my soul in L.A.

--Gloriana Casey

FOR BRIAN THORPE

I had fallen asleep early the night of his death, and then awoke shortly after deciding to check facebook. It was a shock to see Brian's name and "died" in the same post. I remembered him as vital and very alive.

I did not know Brian well but remembered his dignity and presence as he volunteered to read in his rich actor's voice, poems others had written. His comments were always sensitive and astute. Of course, it was always special when he decided to read his own work, which was delightful.

Brian had driven me home one day after poetry and, although he was very private, I got a small glimpse of the enormous challenges he had overcome and still had to deal with. I was reminded of my boyfriend who had passed away a year earlier – both were writers and actors and both gifted. Both men had struggled against a system that did not understand its poets and dreamers, and a system that did not make room for them. And, like Jack, he too had thrown away his mortal constraints and entered into the blue, blue sky.

a cool breeze
passing through
and then no more

--Peggy Castro

Originally published in *What the Wind Can't Touch: Southern California Haiku Study Group Anthology, 2016.*

46

SPRING'S BEGINNINGS

It had been a short winter. A few weeks of rain and then the weather beginning to warm. I was at my favorite garden thinking of Jack, my boyfriend who had died over a year ago, thinking of a flirtation I had with the Irish businessman at the monastery – thinking of all the daddies who never came through.

Suddenly I looked up. There were several hawks circling slowly in the blue sky looking for prey. A breeze passed through. Suddenly I felt safe. I knew I had come home to myself, free from predators. I could feel the blossoms bursting inside of me, ready to bloom in magnificent colors.

signs of Spring
my frozen heart
once a liability
returned home to me
safe in the garden

--Peggy Castro

AUTUMN MEMORIES

In the rose garden
proudly blooming flowers
lifted their burgundy lids indifferently
to the deafening nine o'clock bell
and "fight on" song in my head
their beauty not perceived
in my stark mood

I had returned to that charade
from the desperate, neon lit streets
where I hooked up with strangers
with a sales speech learned from
Taipei's lower class, underground population
I am from America
would you like to know English
here on this street

Reborn in September
I strolled to the liberal arts building
where I had raised my hand
and juxtaposed Woolf and Wells
saying "they both touched on the human condition
the individual soul versus the crowd" and so on
to head-nodding, praise-giving professors

Passing clusters of smiling sorority girls
I felt enormous shame
that I had walked alone
with my honor society membership
and *Daily Trojan* theatre critic title

--Jackie Chou

OUTSIDE STARBUCKS

The refreshing, elusive wind
on this end-of-summer evening
finds me once again
on the patio of the famed café
surrounded by the usual
coffee-sipping, non-smoking crowd

The breeze
suspends time and thought
making room for a moment of bliss
so seldom experienced now

A carefree mind
is no longer mine

I close my eyes and breathe it all in
forgetting earlier today's heat

--Jackie Chou

SANTA FE, FLAGSTAFF TO BARSTOW
THROUGH THE MOJAVE

How could we leave Hotel Santa Fe
where the tall branches of Arizona Ash
watched from the windows,
leaf-scattered fragments of light on our bodies.
Where, for a little while
Our clothes hung in the closet
while we burrowed together on the third floor.

We stop in Flagstaff,
Yelp invites us to
the coffee house where everyone goes,
red and cream linoleum diamonds
waxed to a patina of nostalgia,
photos of kids' baseball teams.
We are locals for a time-
Our story simple. We met, fell in love and married.
Our years dusted with joy
 in the city that never cut down it's trees.

You're staring at your cell phone
plotting the route home.
(I see those checkered tiles, the mismatched furniture
when I sit in my kitchen
in Los Angeles.)

We watch the land between.
Startling white clouds, monsoon thick,
rolling on the horizon, edges burning
against the violet blue sky
always ahead of us.

The asphalt hi-way pulls us forward.
I wedge into the red leather seat,
watch the clouds parade
and read to you. You watch the white line
to keep us safe and get us home.

I'm reading, "Sonny's Blues"
about music creating a sacred landscape
making a home in a harsh land.

The light is changing us
so we will always want to return.
80 miles an hour-
Why are you going so fast?
I never want to get to Barstow
Slow everything down again.

--Marsha Cifarelli

BUSYNESS AS USUAL

Benumbed by the usual business of life
is the lot of too many. Distracted, engrossed,
never lifting our eyes from our self-imposed trifles,
we flit like nits fleeing a fast-fading host,

take no time for ourselves, till too soon we too die --
some by God, some by Man, some by self, most by merely
an uncaring Nature -- and we but survive
when instead we could *live* without paying so dearly.

Getting, begetting, forgetting the pounds,
must we drudge through our days taking care of the pence,
and with little or nothing to show for it? Zounds!
Why would anyone trudge through a life with no sense?

But today we've our chance, we may yet have our druthers:
One sure-shining day may redeem all the others.

--Stephen Colley

THINK THRICE

To think through an issue is tough,
so don't think you can think off the cuff.
Though you're not quite a dunce
if you think only once,
I'm afraid your first thought's not enough.

For a first thought's just rolling the dice,
and on second thought won't seem so nice.
Every instant reaction
is ripe for retraction.
Far better for you to think twice.

And though second thoughts sound the alarm,
simply resting there often does harm.
You may still come to naught
without one more last thought.
When thinking, the third time's the charm.

--Stephen Colley

UNCLAIMED

When we gaze at the heavens, it should
be equal-opportunity-ogling. The citizens
of Mars are dreamed of; those famous Martians.

Are we blameless there are few stories of Uranus
beings? Uranian stars are nameless? They are
unnoticed occupants with acknowledgment needs
completely ignored as we looked past them.

We gave our time and rallied attention to the
declassification of Pluto

Well Pluto doesn't care, has its own measuring
stick and knew to keep a dark distance from Earth.
Pluto noticed Earth while mankind was a thought
floating in a cloud of dust.

Pluto watched Earth before humans formed two eyes
to look at the sky. Pluto knew Earth was round back
when humans believed it to be flat.

In Pluto's classification book, the other bodies in our
solar system do not have beings on it fighting.
Neptune's turbulence is organic and sees Pluto's
point. Venus strongly agrees, Mars is tired of our
explosions, Uranus is not our ally (because of our
treatment) believes we need to go "get-a-moon."

They all "rock-out" in agreement. War makes
Earth not a planet!

--Beverly M. Collins

WICKED CANOPY

This night is much like
wind graffiti moving across
a name that rain cannot banish.

Where one floats facedown in a pool
of memories with every sense open
to the sweet and gritty that welcomes
wicked ways.

Feeling guilty as a green fly alone
with an uncovered cake,

I borrow the ways of water.
Wear away rock just one small
drip at a time.

Move with transparency and laugh.
Cause the streetlamps nervousness.
Part the city like the sea. Every step,
new ground claimed.

--Beverly M. Collins

BREAKAGE / HAVING A DAY

I wanted an invisible tiny pill for
the big headaches. The kind one
could swallow with ease without
a forethought or an aftertaste.

I gave myself a time-out,
a tune-out and an unplug.
A period where I could
move through meadows and chase
butterflies that crossed the
daydreams that I conjured.

Not much to ask for healing time away
from the donut life; middle missing
parts visible appear-to-be-glazed.
I looked myself in a mirror and unfriended.

I wanted to chill just right without
freezing out flavors that I've warmed
up to...wanted to simmer down to a
lukewarm that suited the burnt-out palate.

By the end of my timeout, I had forgiven
myself of all transgressions with a clear
mind. I looked myself in the same mirror
and turned the other cheek. Sent myself
a text that I should stop by for dinner.

Grabbed me with both hands from the
lost and found. There is nothing warmer
than a rekindle with one's own self.

--Beverly M. Collins

"JUST IN CASE"
(For Linda, a mom)

Today, you might just find
Those moments you lost.
You know the ones you packed up
For a rainy-day depression

Problem is Ms. Depression, ever a
Wiley trickster
Hides them on those days

Your back-up position
Tattoos a list on your forearm,
Ms. Depression
Makes you shiver and the
Extra sweater covers that
Ink stopgap

Guru Nancy, at suicide hot line, gives
You her # just in case, but
Yep, you
Zipper
It inside your wallet
And forget it's there

You look at your options –
Smile, you forget how
Eat, no fun any more
Make-up, why bother?

Staring into space, you
Realize you're
Bored of it all –

Underneath lives a wet
Fleshy wound
That needs a voice.

The phone rings-
"Hello, Mom. I'm depressed."

Sometimes it's not up to us
To fight,
She's there. You know.
Just in case.

--Devo Cutler-Rubenstein

MOMENT

In the heartbeat of your silence,
I find rest—
a reprieve from the chaos
of my wild mind.
In a hurricane of beauty
with furious force, you
are stillness in the center,
where black tears flow clear
like virgin snowmelt streams—
where the song of the sparrow
shines brighter
than ten thousand stars.

--Stacy DeGroot

SHE WAITED

I remember that day well.
He made me lie down in green pastures, next to still waters.
So at peace was I, in the cool green grass, that I closed my eyes
and smiled, to await his kiss. He laughed and made me promise
not to peek, to trust our love, always— he would come for me.

Hours passed, and then days. Games of delight, darkened
with the rise of the moon— he didn't come.
Refusing to believe, refusing to not too, I gave my life away
and allowed the earth to swallow, as time does, our lost love.

Now I'm back to the place we started, where there is no trace
of our love once loved, save a ragged wooden cross carved,
"She Waited." And now I understand what that girl never could—
that even though he never came, one day— I would.

--Stacy DeGroot

WHEN I SMOKED PENCILS

It started at night
when I would write
ill until
my instrument would alight
and alight
and smoke —
brought it up to my mouth,
inhaled,
I toked,
tickled by the taste of lead,
the unadulterated *shhh*,
No. 2,
unfiltered,
short bus color coated
sweet chicory cudgel,
charred chopstick —
airy balsa,
cedar, unscented,
juniper, amalgamated
particle pulp,
the better the sharpening,
the shaving,
splintered shards
splaying,
nervous impressions,
incisive vampire marks
stabbing, sucking
my areol's,
my bronchioles,
the nipples
slicing through my chest —
an ecstasy of contractions,
a shiver of the esophagus,
ill until
I coughed blackened flecks,

squiggles —
little corrections in red —
the last thing I wrote
when I smoked
pencils.

--Seven Dhar

Originally published in *The Coiled Serpent: Poets Arising from the
Cultural Quakes and Shifts of Los Angeles*, an anthology by the Los
Angeles Poet Laureate Luis J. Rodriguez's Tia Chucha's Centro Cultural,
distributed by Northwestern University Press.

LOONEY'S DREAM

As the stars started to get brighter
the encampment seemed to grow
meaner it seemed like a bad
spirit had slithered under a fence
shadows began to moan and
laughter became evil growls

The last thing I heard anyone say
was said by a man named Looney

Looney was from the east coast
had been homeless since
the age of 15 said he moved to California
because it got too cold in the winter
to be sleeping out doors

On this night in sunny California
Looney stood next to a cardboard box
drinking from a large can of old English beer

With both arms raised into the air
like some kind of lost king
he says loud enough for
the whole encampment
to hear

He says—

"This is my slice of the American dream, so don't any of you bozos
mess with it"

I had a long drive ahead of me and work in the morning
Next time I'll bring my sleeping bag and a tarp
It seems like there's still more

to
see
touch
and to be
felt by

--Marvin Louis Dorsey

GOD OF SALT AND STONE*

As I am lowered into the earth
and sink into that which came before
deep beneath the soil a voice resounds
We're still H E R E
*Nothing has change*d

We're just not up there anymore
There's lots to do
write books and poems
draw and paint
even fall in love

Some of them tell stories
about their past lives
laughing at their mistakes
saying it's all fine now
just a little dusty
You get used to it

Now they're singing to me
It's a strange song
a cross between a dirge and a jig
Their last words are delivered
with gleeful exuberance
Welcome to the underworld

The first thing I do
is blow my nose

--Pauli Dutton

---

*Title of a collage by Toti O'Brien

CLOSE THE DOOR

Finally settled
sleeping satisfied
until awakened
by a shrill voice commanding
--Open your secrets
Please let me be I pray
Who wants truth to disturb
her quietude?

--Not I say the flowers soundly sleeping
--Not I say the horny goat weed
rustling in the wind
--Let us be lonely
--Let us be unhappy
--Just let us be

If I listen to you
what will happen to my familiar?
Please don't open me
Just let me be
A silly saint illuminated by moonlight
not a ravaged hag
loosened by your twisted forgiveness
lowered by the black mulch of your breath
slowly slipping into…

Close the door
Cover the peep hole
I don't want to know the details
I'd rather sleep--dream myself
inside an Impressionist painting
The hard lines of your world
inhabit an inner sanctum
Leave me live amidst spirits

while you gallop with ghosts
tracking in the mud

Days of shrieking prayer
followed by light
then darkness
I thought we had opened up the sky
Why are you closing it again?
How dare you lock away my heaven!

--Pauli Dutton

THE LAST MERMAID

Sliding through an underwater world
undulating gray and green
I wrap myself in a scarf
of turquoise and teal

the only colors I allow close to me
A translucent six petaled star
swims past a sea of grasses
as they lie down to make way

The silent floor
presents a deceptive
sense of peace
Still there is delight

in joining
the jellyfish ballet
diving in the company of turtles
riffing with the whales

Yet these too will cease
dissolve or drift away
like everything
that matters

So here I remain
until the end of me
and my kind
when this essence

melds with my
mermaid sisters
dancing into the effervescent
white bliss

--Pauli Dutton

SOUND OFF / FACE OFF

People don't have names now
Their name was the key to opening them up
They have faces
Over time they disguise themselves

Faces can tell a lot
But a friend wants to be able to
Include sound to spill emotions
Telephone works better than silent video

Software recognizes face and voice
It translates speech to text or to commands
Computers in pencils correlate student's notes
With audio of the professor's voice

Talk to programs faceless (so far)
Or to humans of face-book or video
See earth from orbit
Your abode from different views

The computer is a brain extension
For memory storage communication
We are part of the world brain
(Accessible by voice for less reading)

Has Big Brother spread or caught
Knowledge viruses from the web
Broadcast with evil or good intent?
Too many media police watching you?

Are they changing A.D. to A.I.?
Expert systems can guide the Media-ocracy
The battleground is communication
Design babies can be DNA'd to accept the message

Will octuplet youngsters tweet on twitter?
Get together or order frozen embryos?
Part of that is late for my generation
Unless they had feel-o-vision suits

Where are my hearing aids?
Can YOU hear ME now?
Umm…What's your name?
God, is that really your face?

--Richard Dutton

"ELECTRIC"-AL OR "BIO" LOGICAL CARE-EARS

popups down food even chew ally
it's over pop … you lay shunned
re-sources were where

"elect trick" "gov buy the people"
people buy the "elect trick" gov
or both
worse ship media?
web flix minister
privacy obsolete

I.T. mob-rule evolves
less parlor men teary pro seed "jars"
poll lease "can" due wit

slow invasion of flocks
changes politics
but watts a bout fast A.I. into I.T?

robe arts: …... pay: ……. off …….
are we above swarm theory insects
who co-op for eatables they find?

can GMO humans keep
leadership rules
over A.I. and I.T.

poll lie tickle puppet stars
leave couch potato minds
in orbit chew airy

butt don't dwell on rear ends
look a-head "four words" to a
human better "plan it"

spending our lives
bee-ing together is a
good buy and better bio

--Richard Dutton

THE ELECTRIC HEATER

To make it through the day
At home I have an electric heater
She warms my life in every way
She's so good you can't beat her
She knows when my power is low
She's also an electric meter
She charges me up so I can go
I always say, "I love you." when I greet her
Ever since so long ago
I was so happy to meet her

--Richard Dutton

Originally published in *Looking Out of Alhambra: A Poetry Anthology*, 2005.

SHE RUNS TO THE EDGE OF TIME IN PINK STILETTOS

A persistent waxing gibbous moon hisses across the sky.
Hungry rivers mist *colla parte* at her lips.
Shall I write your obit while drinking black coffee with cream or
red tea with honey?
Which high-backed chair is closest to the horizon?
Your lazy profiterole sits on the plate, smiling.
We've both lost patience for men with indigo hands.
The city sleeps even though the bridge is luminous with illusions.
My girdle shines sadness through its hands like a sweet pea on the vine.
Pass the persimmons, you said in June, winking like a semaphore.
I opened her jewelry box and heard the sound of a cricket, slowed to a psalm.

--Alicia Elkort

Originally published in *Arsenic Lobster*, April 2017.

SAVIOR

At the horizon we pray
  our fears, beseech the flickered foam.

        A boat in the distance
not a boat

        forty seconds, sixty? an eternity
before she bares down ...

But she slips beneath the water
                lifts us
                from this brackish spray

rises her body
        through a halo of cloud—

our boat a shiver
of splinters balancing
upon her spine, so close

        I touch her whale skin
smooth at thirty knots,

                her eye looking through
a lacey trail of sky.

When finally we understand
        our prayers, mute with thirst and surrendered
                to ocean,

        forgiveness on our lips like salt,

she lets us down at the shore
        jeweled with miles of green—

                mangrove, palms, ferns, magnolia....

Waves crash a hymn
                across the sand. We bless her

        with our milky breath,

                hum our own
                salvation.

--Alicia Elkort

74

GALAXIES

Is the woman
walking in the woods
finding firewood
     or celebrating trees.

Is the man
selling oranges
remembering her touch
     or grateful for symmetry.

The child laughing
in her father's arms
is she imitating those around her
     or has she glimpsed the edge of love.

I want to give to you
the slivered stars
in the sky-are they real the
stars above the moon
in the faded sky –
is the light an illusion
of distance?

How we center and focus
on the details of our lives,

as if collecting bits
makes us mighty.

How we love our dark
roast coffee with two
teaspoons of sugar not three,
clinking the spoon against
the cup so not one drop
is lost, and all the while,
we are stardust.

You want to count petals.
I want to speak of infinity.

--Alicia Elkort

ODE TO MY MOTHER

You were born from the desert. The night sky spit you up and waited until your infinite space found its place in the ground. You weaved throughout the dirt like a root and rose a flower. When the surface finally arrived you found your shelter on a camel's back and drank the wine the locals gave you. You drifted through the wind like a gypsy on your own. You didn't flee You flew. Place to place. Wandering eye. It saved you. And from there you were given the strength you possess. Beauty only you can hold. Like a goddess worthy of worship. You took the dark back from the earth and hammered it down with light. Now you glow. Controlling the elements with one sleight of hand returning to the roots like and ancient warrior. You are mighty.

--Lowam Eyasu

DEFY POETIC CONFUSION

Do not confuse a light-ish touch
With one where there is not so much to say
Just because some words like to play
For lyrical invective is not the only means to be effective
When one merely needs to be reflective
And taking out parts necessary will only make the whole defective
Do not confuse a twinge of whimsy
With lack of substance, with being flimsy
Do not confuse stylish depravity
As lending forth an air of gravity

Do not confuse a little rhyme
Rocking back and forth in time
As lacking erudition or an embarrassing condition
Which should be banished to perdition
After all, rhyme has tradition

Do not confuse a lack of sadness
As embracing stylistic badness
Do not confuse anomaly
Reaching some complexity
Not fashioned from perplexity
With an homily teaching non neutrality
Upon a thought about morality
In conclusion
Defy confusion

--Lynn Fayne

PILE OF FEATHERS

One feather lifts from the pile
like abandoned bonfire ash
after sharp tooth snarl,
and a whack on the head,
the surviving chickens
wandering the pen's perimeter
crying obscenely
as my son places bricks
over the mound.

This death, another.
It is nature. It is animal to die.
Not evil. Though death
feels that way
when it comes suddenly,
when it has another body
to blame no matter
the connection, the instinct.

Doubt bleeds:
the neck wilts when lifted,
the eye still under translucent lid,
a gate left unlatched --
entrails of what-if
left in absence.

The bones break
under the weight of moist dirt.
The worms move in to live.
We eat the last eggs
in solemn ceremony --
the dark yokes

pooling on our plates --
while the dogs lay at foot
hiding their bloody snouts
beneath paws.

--Emily Fernandez

CALIFORNIA ANGEL

An angel abides
at the Luna Motel
on the lonely end of wormhole time
where the landscape's crucified
        by the crossroads
of midnight Cadiz
along the dark highway
where her hitchhiking began

Nothing new
in that creosote and sand
save rusty tin cans beneath
        the yucca trees
and ancient black rocks
covered with pictographs
        and spray paint
as white bloomed datura
        like lilies grow

Once Beat poets
burning in a fever
pounded out the rhythm of the road
in engines and tires
hauling loads of angels and Okies
singing blacktop hymns
not heard anymore

And the angel
dances beneath uncounted stars
across the vast
empty stretches of road
        where the truckers no longer go
to shatter solid doubt beneath
        a veneer of conviction

and the spectrum hosts
        no pirate radio
to rant of forgotten destiny
and spout its midnight religion
full of pious preening
but only the silence of despair

But still she waits
by the side of the road
at the old Luna Motel
waiting for lauds
and a ride –
        to take her back to heaven

--Mark A. Fisher

THE SKY WAS IN THE EARTH

they let their wings down
standing in a row
on a hill above the city
they walked barefoot
through the forests
into the quiet streets
while the people slept
they entered
a house, a man, dark hair
sat beside him on the bed
gently pulled the linen sheets
and put their hands
on his soft throat
while in his dream he felt
he was a girl, crouching
at river's edge, the sun
was white with rage
as he as she dipped fingers
into cool water
stirring up still things that lay unseen
they touched his head and let him dream
and left the way they came
in darkness
on the stairs a dog looked on
as they stepped lightly past
and did not bark
for angels do not move
as humans do

--R. Ford

CIEN AÑOS FAMILY SITE

Crossing the border from Arizona to California
Blythe smelled like summer watermelons grown
beyond ripe yet left to lie putrid in waste fields

Water from our Aunt Lavinia's front yard pump
like Hades halitosis reeked same offensive odor
What soiled determinant, what dirty armpit this?

Was it the mighty red clay of the Colorado?
Land along its banks held limitless water rights
binding families as hell-hole-hostages-in-perpetuity

Most awful offal scent, like hi-desert turkeys, has
evaporated since terra fertile now produces not food
but subsidized Section-8 convict family housing

The few remaining consolidated farmers still plant
 high thirst crop-seed like alfalfa, cotton, cantaloupe,
tomatoes, watermelon, and rice for fruitful bottom line

-- G T FOSTER

MOON POEM 1

Poem,
finally you came
dressed in night
and I made you woman
to see if it suited you.

That's why I gave you
the moon as diadem
and the stars
to play with.

And, with your words
in my mouth,
my eyes closed
and I went to sleep.

--Elsa Frausto

❧

MOON POEM 2

In the three o'clock of the morning,
the moon wakes me up.
I say the moon because no one else is around.
Oh, la luna, with her closely cropped hair
and the muted blue light of her face.

Changeable, true to her appearance, disappearance.
See! Outside same as inside,
no genie in this bottle.
Just bottle
filling up with her.

--Elsa Frausto

THE THORNS OF THE JOURNEY

Close to death
I lost consciousness
Thorns waited for
 me
Like a fox waiting to pounce upon a chicken.
Even as my brain swelled and bled,
Somewhere my brain was fighting;
Thorns waited for me.
I awoke one day;
I was aware of every thought, every action.
The thorns waited for me.
I retreated to the safety of a life in limbo
Evading the senseless reality I faced;
I could not embrace the journey that waited.
And the thorns waited for me;
They simply waited for me.
Weeks went into the journey;
I used the thorns to feel again;
The thorns waited for me,
And I put one foot in front of the other
To resume the journey
To complete the journey
To make the waiting thorns useful
Those thorns became my stepping stones.

--Martina Robles Gallegos

OCTOBER ELEVENTH

Our home turned to ice one bitter cold night,
winter rattling the door before we knew it.
Withered witch fingers hung from the threshold
admonishing our foolish contentment,
fractures in the floorboards held us hostage
when our propriety became too heavy.
White breath puffed out, visible, hovering
silence where the words that should have been said were not.

--Damian Gonzalez

THE JOY OF COOKING

I have tears in my eyes
But not from cutting onions
I'm laughing out loud
But not from jokes in my cookbook
Oil is sizzling and hot
But pan remains empty
Not all the cooking wine
Makes it into the pot

I want to cook for you
I want you in my kitchen
My spice box is exploding
Hot chili peppers set hearts on fire
Curry burns holes in souls
Lips blister from sampling salsa
Sweet and sour

What strange alchemy transforms
Simple ingredients into life?
Miracle food, magical energy source
Gives strength to go on
Neither Woman nor Man
Can live by bread alone
We both need something more
Something hearty that endures
That sticks to Adam's ribs
Also Eve's
A great big serving
Of passion and romance.

I'm dishing that up
With a chef's flair for cuisine
Words of love to nourish
Hungry hearts and thirsty souls

It's hot and spicy and ready…
Are you hungry too?
Care to join me?

--Charles Harmon

Previously published in *Spectrum 4, 2016's Top Ten San Gabriel Valley Poets,* April 2016.

LOVER

After a long day at the office
I climb in my car and drive fifty miles
in rush hour traffic

As I reach my exit off the San Diego Freeway
my pulse quickens, sweat moistens my hands
I am getting closer to the moment
I've been waiting for all day

I pull into the garage,
grab my purse
jump out of the car
open the door and rush into the bedroom
to find you still lying on the bed
where I left you this morning

I pull my clothes off
climb between the sheets and pull you close
gently, stroking your back
I open your covers
and devour
every word

--Hazel Clayton Harrison

Originally published by *TA Publications,* Minneapolis, MN, 1992.

A KIND OF YEARNING

Anne's face, tilted to the side,
clung to the pillow, just enough
to face the window. The
grey gaze of October held her
with cold hands.

Her long, thin neck
stretched,
twisted
tendons tight just to give me casual commands.

I folded laundry as the only favor I could do.

T-shirts in the middle drawer,
underwear in the top and
pants too loose fitting
up into the closet
with everything else that
was worn out and faded.
Banished reminders, piled out of sight.

I looked at her
look past me, out
to some dandelion trail,
beyond the window.

A kind of yearning, a giving in to the quiet,
that we, in silence, named strength.

The funhouse mirror truth
stretched,
twisted
until only an optimistic outlook stood.

Now.
The city spreads across the dark
like shattered, glistening glass and
I know without reflection, the
look on my own face.

--David Humphreys, Jr.

S.E.R.A.P.H.

Mine is a bit twisted
with a lazy eye and no teeth.

She never learns, my dear angel of scars and scumbags,
my dead hummingbird on high heels.

Ah! My G.A. is a real sin-machine, working off 10,000
indecencies, 8,700 lies, 2,500 false promises and 285 murder fantasies.

In short, I am doomed.
No rest for the wicked, as the cliché goes.

Could be she accrued a credit balance in the afterlife
by selling off bits and pieces of her soul while still alive.

Until then, she is my Super-Erotic, Retro-Angelic, Post-Human.
(S.E.R.A.P.H. for short.)

My dead diva is barely hanging on, doing her best
to keep me alive day after day.

That's no easy task, I assure you.
She pulled the shortest straw.

I am a danger zone of civil wars and orange cones,
an autobiography of drunken tirades and suicidal thoughts in the shower.

Wouldn't you "die" to protect me?
Yes, my angel, she keeps on tickin'

although, as luck would have it,
she's 20 minutes late for every bad decision.

--Armine Iknadossian

OF LOVE AND OCTOPI

I try to think it through,
but thoughts have many limbs.

They flail and grab and recede.
They suction off a piece of peace,

grab at the capstone heart,
shade the love-light from one's eyes.

One arm pushes him away.
One arm pulls him close.

Two arms hold his
beautiful, trembling hands.

Another wonders about
the dead, the living
and those in between.

The sixth one is tethered
to the craggy depths of sorrow.

The seventh fights off
morays of doubt.

The eighth arm,
camouflaged against coral,

waits for the right time
to unfurl like a new leaf.

--Armine Iknadossian

I REFUSE TO GET OLD

Spring awakens the earth,
gives hope for regeneration.

I refuse to get old,
play catch with the racing flow

of time. I know the law of life:
immutable as translucency of rain.

Born into this world
I don't know any other.

Dawns and sunsets
continue into infinity,

ideas burst forward -
we advance.

The muse sings lyrics
to my stanzas, offers me
a thimble of immortality.

--Gedda Ilves

HIGH STAKES

You love me so much
                 lifetime lifeline
Lost my way
                 detoured disappeared

We do not recognize us
                 I miss me you
Let's
                 SEE each other.

--Gerda Govine Ituarte

IN THE LIGHT OF US

Glimpse his face
Boyish charm captivates

Eyes caress me
Camera in hand
Stand over there

Turn your head right
Raise eyes chin slightly
Gimme that smile

Click
Back up little more to the left
Throw shawl over shoulder

Click click
My baby looks sexy
Sometimes he flirts

Mi Amor Mi Vida Mi Corazón
We laugh he spins me around
In the light of us.

--Gerda Govine Ituarte

WORDS TO BUTTERFLIES

Words find their
way out.

I am silence
space light.

Words to page.
Hands butterflies.

--Gerda Govine Ituarte

STAY— SHE RISES IN THE SUNSET

I'd forgotten I was soft
I'd forgotten I was pensive
I'd forgotten to make time for affection
- Its sleepless seductions and asexual submissions -
With allowances to reflect my humorous senses

I'd forgotten I was beautiful
I'd forgotten I was bold
I'd forgotten how to get lost in my cauterized present
-Its urgent curiosity despite dusty eyefuls -
Without losing my bleeding soul

But then I exercised my ostracized inner child
And found her even more resilient yet
And her dimensions rose to the surface like a second skin
- Their rising brilliance against shadows, stained -
When, surrendering to its reign, I stayed for the sunset

--Lisa'Anne G. Ivey

VIOLENCE

It could happen
when I use his coffee cup
for my orange juice
or when I ask a question
during the football game
or wake him
when he overslept
it could happen
when I cause a paper jam in the printer

but when I tell him
he killed my love
how he shouted it away
then he is suddenly silent
and I wonder if the violence
of his words
will transfer
to the gun under our bed

--Kathleen Jacobson

SCHOOL DAYS

My memory
is redder than meat
silent witness
to bloody walks home
dodging landmines
and 5th grade bullies
hurling insults
nicknames that pierce
the heart
even time
cannot wipe clean
the damage

--Kathleen Jacobson

TURN OF A KEY: HYPOCRITIC

The nursing home reeked of old medicine, sick and sweet
As decomposing hope
A mask for waiting, limbo of misery
Locked in its antiseptic fumes

She was at my elbow and I, unaware,
Focused on retrieving necessaries, safeguarding valuables
My thoughts a few miles distant with him
Locked away in ICU
A barrier of glass and terror

Her face was a Yukon Gold smashed into puffy fury
The color of her teeth
Beady eyes like rodents' snapping
As she hissed a venomous litany
How he had yelled at her
He, deaf, locked in solitary pain
Striving to reach her stuffed and selfish ear

I heard myself mouth platitudes,
Wanting to cap her valve of complaints
Complete my task
And go to his side
He might be awake
Unlocked
Maybe he would be able to hear me
She was a fly of annoyance

I nodded, I tried to smile
That pinched fullness of tears
In my nostrils
I collected what I needed
One foot after another down that sepulchral fluorescent hall
And went away
Hoping to see him smile

He passed two weeks later
And I think she was Death
With coffee breath and nasty words
Come to prepare me for pain

--Briony James

THE DISTAFF SIDE

We pull and ease the threads between fingers
Sensitized by the waves
Washing over our years

Waves that ebb and flow and jostle us
Flotsam we drift
Jetsam we jettison

Our feelings, thoughts, selves
Biting hard into nagging tongues
To still true words

Our Cinderella slippers are adept
We tight walk our way through lives
That leave us wondering

Melting into tomorrow's
Necessities

Practical collisions of dreams
Against real rocks
Amid words
Acts
Violations

We learn to not respond
But never ignore
Never off guard

You are not trustworthy
We learn that very fast

And go through life at your sides
Wary
Wondering
When?

--Briony James

HARMONIUM

a drone, constant and companionable
like the soft buzz of afternoon bees,
the sounds of your breath
soft snore, sometimes raucous,
requiring a gentle elbow
to remind you I need sleep

moonlight pours mercury light
over our dreams, the busy bees,
our hopes, the midnight birdsongs echoing
in diurnal bustle when we pause,
smile over late day tea,
and let nightmagic wash into end of day,
a watercolor of time

--Briony James

BETTING ON THE BIG BANG

The stars were kicking up a fuss after
a bad weekend on the sports front.
The wrong teams had won again.
It was the planets that had their
glad--even radiant for some--faces on today.
I didn't want any part of the argument.
I wanted to merely clean up the curves
on my morning depression and get on with my day.
Why should any of us have to get in
the middle of a Milky Way melee?
Some of these stars can be real babies
about it all—holding a grudge for light years.
They should know by now that the odds
are rarely in their favor—not to say that
the universe is fixed and plays favorites.
Moons seem to always get the short straw.
Asteroids never get a fair shake.
And it goes on and on out there in deep space.
I have my own planetary problems thank you very much.
There is no reason to go looking for a celestial skirmish.
There are enough unhinged ideas floating
around in my own Earth's atmosphere.
It may be weightless out there, but all the petty
grudges can certainly drag a person down.

--Jeffry Jensen

Originally published in *Spectrum 4* 2016, Don Kingfisher Campbell, editor.

WE ARE, I AM

I'm a mouthpiece for many.
My family has a deep history with more generations to come.
So many hold prejudice, but we're the type to hold none.
We adapt: no matter the cost or how big the loss.
Down for the cause, a rebel without a pause.
We respect the laws, but sometimes we're called upon to break it.
Doing what has to be done. We see past race, color, creed, peace, and hatred.
I'm not a bully. I'm not.
But sometimes I get so engrossed with power I impose my will.
Whether it's to make sure the point gets across or just for a cheap thrill.
We aren't some forgotten tribe or a group that dwindled in size.
Sometimes we're forced out of our homes, but we're very much alive.
We move in every town just looking for a spot to call our own.
We should be left alone; allowed to protect our homes.
Your kids even know us, but often times they see us and run.
Rarely drowned out by silence when we catch them one by one.
They keep putting the blame on us because of all the wrongs we've done.
They don't want to take responsibility for the monster they've created,
for I'm merely a gun.

--Patrick Jimenez

KENSINGTON CONCIERGE

At 3:00 a.m. I'm wide open as the window.
The moon offers what little light it has
bringing London's ghosts – stray thoughts

of streetwalkers climb the flues,
and take root. This room holds its hurts –
swollen feet, bent neck, the width of the lift

when you looked in me. Some part of us rose
to the surface then silvered as it sank.
An odd pull, like a thread

in the underwing, but I kept
from touching your velvet yarmulke,
rubbed my voice for a path to speak.

I know you. You are dark oil
in a new lamp and even if you give your days
to the opening of doors

or the recovery of what we lost –
a red glove or a gentleman's cufflink,
my leather diary full of words of you

left on the clean sheets, you are still my keeper
of the lantern and there's only this pale hour
illumining your raven suit, its cotton so close

to my fingers. I've only had one tryst in my life,
but Levi I would break the rule for you –
break it like matzo on a candled night. I want

to hear you explain the strange razor calls
of rooftop birds, our vowels rain-lipped. You are
the kind of man who looks with your whole body.

Come here in your night coat like a Cossack.
Come in – your dark curls still, untouched.

--Lois P. Jones

Previously published in *Wide Awake: Poets of Los Angeles and Beyond
(Pacific Coast Poetry Series),* March, 2015.

RED HORSE

No one understood this blood run
to the moon, this blaze

of you, red horse in a swollen sky.
How you turned loose

like a fistful of fire ants.
How your temper could burn

a field when there was too much
to drink. There were days we'd spread

the blanket on the grasses
near the sycamores and let the desert

air run through us,
let the sage burn our nostrils

as we sipped a silky rioja.
A wine you liked to translate,

as you decoded everything beautiful.
Your lips full and slightly curled

siempre, siempre: jardin de mi agonia,
tu cuerpo fugitivo para siempre,

always, always: garden of my last breath,
your body escaped forever,

Lorca in his red shoes
lighting our tongues, lifting

our hips until the sun
turned poppy and burst.

--Lois P. Jones

Previously published in *Cultural Weekly*, February, 2016.

AFTER WAGNER'S PARSIFAL

and the red silk sheets
      surge on stage like Moses'
          engorged sea

after the servants kneel and pray
      as King Amfortas is brought down
          on his bed to the forest lake

to bathe his wound
      after a mother in her scarlet dress
          lures the boy Parsifal to her side

we leave the theater's blackout
      of the senses
          silhouettes exit in spiked heels

and felt hats down the brass bannister
      toward flood lights and the scent
          of stale coffee and fine cigars

a man quotes Hitler in the hall
      one can serve God only
          in the garb of the hero

I think of the well-dressed Nazis
      who committed suicide
          at the end of the war

beyond the black doors of the opera house
      the city's sirens loose in us
          like a virulent disease

--Lois P. Jones

Previously published in *One, Jacar Press*, November, 2014.

GOODYEAR GURU

My doctor says I'm shrinking.
Alarmingly, the measuring stick agrees.
But here inside, where a lifetime of memories reside,
I'm quite the same I've been for umpteen years.

So where on this round earth, could
an inch and a half of me have disappeared?
Did particles wear away as I paced down the halls
on dark sleepless nights with babes in my arms?

Or drop off while walking my daughters to school?
Could I have lost more of me as we traipsed
through large malls in search of *the* dress
for each high school prom?

Did I wear farther down as I hiked mountain trails,
or line danced on high-polished floors?
Could increments have ground away
as I pruned and plucked red roses from

the garden patch I tend near my front door?
Perhaps if I would climb a lofty mountain top,
a Guru there would whisper in my ear,
and say I'm One Big Ring of Tread—

like a Goodyear tire rolling through the years,
leaving parts of me, bit by bit, behind.
The farther I go, the more miles I rove,
the more of me wears thin.

If so—are there footpaths I've imprinted,
with the tread pattern called my life,
weaving through my twists and turns of days
to let me know I'm wearing well?

--Lorelei Kay

PASSAGE HOME

"She's deteriorating fast.
Hurry. Hurry home."

I drive as fast as I dare, covering
the six hundred and eighteen miles
pushing through the California, Nevada,

and Utah deserts toward the blue-shingled
roof on Blair Street where my parents lived
since I was in third grade.

But by the time I arrive at Mom's bedside
to stroke her pale red hair and whisper,
"I love you, Mom," she doesn't know
I am here.

I help Dad bathe her with bubble bath
lacing the water, this rag doll of a mom
who used to bathe me.

After Dad carries her back to bed,
I help him dress her, and inhale
the aroma of her bubble bath,

like the lilacs that burst out
in profusion each spring
in front of their home.

And the lilac scent
keeps the smell
of death away,
one day at
a time.

--Lorelei Kay

ALTADENA, 1992

presentiment...
a nervous shiver
passes over
the sleeping rooms
doves on the powerline
murmur together
sidestep
restless...
I wake to the dawn
backlighting the tree line...
no...
not the dawn...
the light comes too early
windchimes are jangling
smoke filters in
through locked down louvers,
waking crazed instinct
adrenaline jerks me
up to the window as
smoke
stains the sunrise
Fire!
somewhere near...
east of Verdugo
south of Chilao,
cresting the ridges
a terrible heat
the blast of its hunger
hollows the meadow
the poppies
the mustard
cringe to the subsoil
firestorms roar over
leave night
like a scar
and all day the ashes
of somebody's treasures

sift down on the parking lots,
drift against
plate-glass...
this strange confetti
this tragic snow

-- lalo kikiriki

ARACHNID IN MY LAMPSHADE

Spider with the tiny body
I watch from my pillow
as you stretch long legs
checking out your lovely gauzy web

You wrap
some hapless prey
in spider silk
ready it for your next meal

Your spindly legs
must tire
from holding your body so still
as you hang upside down

I think sometimes
that you have died
gone to the great spider heaven
in the sky

What think *you*
from your perch
on that diaphanous web
in my lampshade?

Do you feel lucky
that you can work
right there
at home?

Do you look around
wondering
if a mate
will find you here?

Do you dream
about a tasty moth
flying unwittingly
into your sticky web?

Can you see me
just beyond where you are?
Do you wonder
about me too?

--Mina Kirby

WEIGHT

Those days
the weight of stones
undermines
even the sky
calling to the moon,
her sister the sun
gazes
relentlessly
searing a shadowless embrace
upon my soul
marking time
in silver lines
and fishing weights

--Cybele Garcia Kohel

CLOUDS

The first time death visited our generation
it was on a Good Friday, still frozen in Minnesota
but freeways lined with California poppy
short sleeve weather here.

    Easter lilies
    the potted plant
    with my cousin's name on it

But Roy's holiday was not Easter, it was arsenals
of backyard fireworks independence from work summer heat,
it was hamburgers and ribs on the BBQ, potato salad
and baked beans. Stuck in tradition and the order
of seasons, we ate ham and my aunt's green jello salad,
discussed red-eye flights to Minneapolis.

Passenger lists were sparse, only me and my dad
on tomorrow's flight. There were vacancies around the Easter dinner
table, my sister's family on a Mexican cruise, photos with the captain,
decadent desserts and onboard massages, instead of planning
a funeral trip. Chile rellenos and tacos, horchata and michelada,
we remembered Roy's visit to Mexico where he
and his wife climbed countless Mayan pyramid steps
witnessed the Monarch migration, returning home
to plant his own butterfly garden.

        sweep
       of Monarch clouds
      souls of the dead

--Deborah P Kolodji

LIFECYCLES OF GRIEF

(i)

fresh lavender
near her favorite chair
her scent

(ii)

new grave marker . . .
ants underline
a name

(iii)

selling the house
old apple pie recipe
in an already-emptied drawer

(iv)

the wail of wind
in a barren cemetery
dead flowers

--Deborah P Kolodji

WHAT WOULD MR. DARWIN SAY

about the problem
of the vocal cords?
I picture them stretched
along their voice boxes

like mother's clothesline
taut across our basement
awaiting rainy or wintry days

or like the string
drawn firmly between my
fingers as I made Cat's Cradle,
wove Jacob's Ladder.

Will they become brittle
like unused rubber bands
waiting to snap

at the multitudes
tapping away
together, but apart
in communal quietude
selecting silence?

--Linda Kraai

First published in *A Poetic Body of Work* (CLE Press, 2016).

SPIDER

Every night at dusk
from the edge of the balcony
across the space to the elm tree,
I watch a spider spin an invisible web.

Back and forth he travels,
suspended on his tightrope,
preparing for insects who will drift unaware
into his invisible net, like youth into middle age.

--Kitty Kroger

YOUTH ARE DESTINED

Youth are destined to impatience
with our senior moments.

They don't know they too
will hobble down the path of
memory fickle as a cancelled date,
eyes dim as Aladdin's cave,
knees like crumbling buildings
slated for redevelopment.

Our children are sure
they will never arrive
at this dead end of
tangled brain cells,
bodies unraveling
like Watergate.

They are destined not to get it.
We love them anyway.

--**Kitty Kroger**

BAR AUBADE
After Amy Gerstler

Don't worry, my sweet, my bleary bearded pet,
your backwoods drawl and waterlogged eyes
as old as the hills, their ancient and charred spring
come back like a chronic disease, a cancer that wastes
but just won't kill. That sick tint picked up by the salt
dusting the shuffleboard is from neon beer signs,
or the squad car humming past like a sleepy beetle,
not dawn's queasy face.

I still reign secure in our sour-smelling underworld,
a lady, a queen, the taps and bottles and mirrors
twinkling like underground stars. Drink one more
with me, something black and rheumy cold,
a tumblerful of Lethe dipped out right here
where she meets the Styx, before her long trip
down continent to our nether provinces, our salty
and poisoned gulfs. An exoplanetary electricity
crackles in the subwoofers; clasp me like a mellow zombie
and samba or foxtrot with me to its aleatory rhythms.
Let's slip out back, and sit, smoking ourselves
into a kind of wild sobriety, red rimmed
sky of eyes. Climb into my pickup truck,
make yourself snug on the rag rug
while I slip behind the giant steering wheel.
Help yourself to the chocolate bars in the glove box.
Let's set out into the salt mist,
my gnarled and everlasting hand
at the world's unsteady helm.

--Sharon Kunde

Originally published in *Deep Water Literary Journal*, Summer 2016.

SWIMMING IN THE OCEAN

She was never taught to swim.
A few lessons one summer,
but it was never taken seriously.
Somehow, she manages to learn to tread water,
figures out how to swim.
All this time she's kept her head above surface
while hoping to be rescued.
No ship in sight in the vast, vast ocean.

--Leah Lagmay

OPPORTUNIST

Backyard bird feeder sways and rocks
with weight of tousling Stellar Jays
who lean forward
feed in unison.
With aggressive flutter
a mockingbird clears them off
gobbles seed with greedy efficiency.

A bully in every crowd, I think
then I'm stunned to see, ten feet away
a Cooper's hawk perched on my neighbor's roof.
I have seen him before, sky-arced, as he rode
thermal crests, but here
he waits, still as death.
Head cocked, bright eye focused
in perfect sight line on the feeder.

He shifts his gaze
we stare eye-to-eye
as he regards me majestic indifference
Calm predator
and unknowing co-conspirator
he, the only one in this triad
confident of his place in the food chain.

--Kathy Leonard

COUNTDOWN

The gurneys glide into the treatment wait-stack
Against that long white wall.
A toad of a Triage nurse barks names and numbers,
The most-mortal first.
She processes us on parchment paper. Relentless pen.
Strong young techs in whites pry open
The heavy gateway doors,
Moving together in formal motion --
I think of minuets, stately new steps
To the old Dance of Death.
Their starched white backs turn away.

I see leaping red flames, smell the stink of sulphur --
This is Dis, Chiron waits. Where's my coin?
I hear the sound of water suck against his oars,
The clink and jangle of metal in his deep black bag.
The centaur smells of toil, the river of scum, rot, ruin.
The new-dead howl.

The families who'd sobbed on shore
File out, flinging old newspapers
Into white bins.

If that demon nurse's ledger
Has dropped to this dank spit,
I'll be loaded next. My number's up.

--Nancy Lind

HAIKU

borrowed blankets
in autumn solitude
Ghost Ranch under the stars*

night-blooming jasmine
leads me home
in the darkness**

--Janis Albright Lukstein

---

*First haiku was originally published in *Geppo,* November 2016.
**Second haiku was originally published in *Mariposa*, Haiku Poets of Northern California, Spring/Summer 2016.

WE VISIT MY MOTHER AT POILEY TZEDEK CEMETERY

She's right where we left her a year ago; the winter
and the rains didn't quite do the job I thought they would.

Another man's gravestone is leaning up against my
grandmother's in a manner I can only guess my grandfather

wouldn't have approved of. We search for evidence of
their parents in this field of the dead that started with

the Scottish whose stones have yielded to the uncleared
weeds of spring. The Jews have made good use of

the lawnmowers of Syracuse and you can see evidence
of ancestors all the way up to where the top of the hill

meets the sky. Our son wanders into an Orthodox
family ceremony. Either an unveiling or *Yahrtzeit*.

He doesn't know, he just sees people and knows
he's one of them.

--Rick Lupert

LIKE MAGIC

Write, she says,
conjure up words like magic and put them on *that* paper.
A wave of the arms a snap of the fingers
and ... you have got to be kidding.
Magic is not that easy.
First of all it's not really magic;
it's more like trickery.
Sure, you wave your arms and snap your fingers
but it's a distraction
from all the hard work and engineering
that go into create the illusion.
And no overnight success stories;
it takes years and years of practice, practice, practice.
If it was so easy they wouldn't call it magic,
they'd call it writing.

--Joe Lusnia

RUST TO DUST

At Gloria Jean's coffee shop in the Burbank mall
Tall high school girls
Wearing Chaminade High School sweat shirts
Hate their French teachers and
Seem to have no purpose
Except to watch their mothers
Order coffee drinks
With names
Baristas cannot pronounce and

Ingredients only Oprah Winfrey
Understands on a good day

The doors close at 9 p.m.
Like everything else around here

Leaving me to wonder if
Time really does serve a purpose
Other than to drag on into infinity
Or merely be

When the word is
Can be defined a million times
It is easy to get caught up in
Thinking and meditating and
Not doing

While I sit
A thousand moments die and
A hundred people find the casket or fire
Causing me to refrain from
Drinking iced coffee and
Feel the genuine weight around me
Like a monk finding his voice

--Radomir Vojtech Luza

HOME

one year, we lived in a room not a house
celebrated Christmas with a branch not a tree
my mother, on her knees, cleaning toilets,
saved her tips to buy gifts
my father and his nostalgic eyes
fixed everything

old bicycles with rusty chains and crooked handlebars
they hushed their screams
so babies could sleep

one year, we packed everything we owned
carried four suitcases across two oceans
said goodbye to our language and land
left our dead and their unattended gravesites

one year, we received welfare checks and food stamps
drove around in hand-me-down cars
and swallowed all the years of longing
to return

--Karineh Mahdessian

UNTITLED

my father cries--often
when he remembers Tehran. he can't escape home;
everything buried beneath rubble and dust. home;
before the war and the daytime night skies
full of stars and bombs.
he remembers his father
the taste of lavash and cheese
the stern mouth of his mother,
a woman too bitter for life.
my father cries--often
when he hears songs, reads Hafiz and Omar Khayyam
he remembers names of employees he supervised thirty years ago
the places he went traveling as a boy.
my father cries--often
when he sees YouTube clips of Iranian teachers
when he sends emails and text messages
in the only language that has ever felt like his.

they tell me
I have my father's eyes.
I, too, cry often.
it's like shedding skin with razor blades and acid baths.
the sorrow never leaves my bones
it simply remains
until I call it
home.

--Karineh Mahdessian

EXILED

under a full moon
surrounded by sage and honey
you lean to kiss my eyes and my skin jumps
you feel how this body yields to your commands
one beckoning finger and all this hard-shell shatters
you bring me guava
offer yourself as present
so I take you
unwrap each hurt
tug gently at your lip
I want to stay here
between your teeth and crooked smile
until gravity no longer exists.
I want to find home inside your mouth
stay until our babies are born
run fingers through thick curls
call you mine over and until
I finally believe it myself.

--Karineh Mahdessian

9th

The last window in the living room rattled
the first time Father played Beethoven's Ninth.

In Beirut, bombs shattered glass panels, and Fathers
taped plastic sheets on every splintered pane.

I didn't hear the guttural bang of the timpani.
Clashing cymbals didn't symbolize the fiery

arrows of Zeus. Low flying jets coined that claim.
I didn't care for the bombastic choir; they drowned

the rat-a-tat-tat of M16s. I sifted through the noise
like a deaf beggar sifting through the trash

and discovering fleshy pomegranate. That's how
I discovered the French horns, so lonely and lost,

buried deep in Beethoven's Ninth.

--Shahe Mankerian

Originally published in *Mary: A Journal of New Writing,* Spring 2017 Issue and
Finalist for the Editor's Prize of Mary.

BRIOCHES

The bakery crowd looted the last
of the loaves. A beggar child
driven by hunger ignored

the falling bombs; he sucked
on rancid raisins stuck
between his teeth.

Pregnant Fatimah didn't mind
the mold on the leftover crumbs;
she devoured them

as she crossed the checkpoint
full of pungent militiamen.
No one noticed the Druze

cabdriver on fire. No one
tasted the difference between glass
shards and sugar beads

piercing the bloated belly
of brioches. A roach crawled
into the barren oven. The broken

baker sat on the curb
and cried because he ran out
of yeast, butter, and flour.

--Shahe Mankerian

Originally published in *These Fragile Lilacs Poetry Journal*, Volume 2, Issue 2,
Spring 2017 & a Runner-Up for First Annual These Fragile Lilacs Poetry Prize.

THE CITY OF LOST CHILDREN

I can't remember how I felt the first time
I hid behind a skirt in Beirut. Boys couldn't

play in the same playground as girls.
When the headmaster didn't pay attention,

we snuck in. I learned girls chewed gum
secretly. I learned they giggled in unison.

I learned they pulled their skirts up to show
more thighs when the boys came near.

When we heard the whistle, we hid under
the staircase, or behind the trashcan,

or the column that held the church dome.
I hid behind a skirt, unshaven, staring

at a pair of dirty ankle socks, completely safe.

--Shahe Mankerian

Originally published in *Forage Poetry Journal,* Volume 1, Issue 3.

I SEE GOD SMILING

I see God smiling
while men pass judgment on each other
with undeniable, unwavering authority.
He smiles patiently while addressed
from angles He does not choose with us.

I see God smiling a vague, unfathomable
smile at those He created in His image
confident in giving them a free choice
to make decisions, go into the world
proliferate and affect each other

He created Cain and Abel,
venomous vipers and innocent lambs
and much more in between.
He must smile sadly
at the results.

--Mira N. Mataric

THE UNCERTAINTY OF RED SHOES

I have a thing
for red shoes;
they're outré, overt,
a trifle licentious,
willing to try anything once.
If you own red shoes
you know what I mean.

Do red shoes appeal
because they whisked Dorothy
out of Kansas cornfields?
Two clicks
red shoes dance
down the yellow brick road
hard travelin' with three flawed men –
one a lowly coward
one without a heart
one without a brain.

Or, do images of red-hot
shoes the evil queen dons
and dances to her death in
as the fairy tale *Snow White* ends
make red shoes seem a bit chancy
for everyday footwear?

The nagging pair in my closet
give me pause–daring
me to wear them.
They make me whine
"Do I look cheap?"
"Do I really want to stress my feet?"

Depending on my mood
these nervy shoes
often wind up staying home
out-smarted by a common pair of Birkenstocks
who know better than to clamor for attention.

--Pat Murphy McClelland

DATELINE CAIRO, LA

Horizontal morning sun
slants across my garden
illuminating irises in demise
heads once royal, purple
as the robes of ancient
Pharaohs, turned to dun
paper furls coiled like
inauspicious asps basking
in honeyed light while
the Nile dreams of overflowing.

Retired irises wrinkled
by heat and time
await recycling
long to emerge
in afterlife as
crinkled papyrus
woven and pressed
into parchment scrolls
for insurgent scribes
conspiring to upend
tradition by filing briefs
of chicanery in high places –
news of old Egypt's spring uprisings
I read in the thinning *LA Times*.

--Pat Murphy McClelland

OLD WOMAN

Old woman sits alone
As the sun sets on her life
She watches television
In her threadbare room
The politics of today blaring
Her arm is wet
The numbers in blue ink there
Are crying

--Alice Meerson

WHISPERS

Whispers across a café table
  Evoke an earlier era
Of jazz filtering through cigarette smoke
And women in slinky dresses
  Whose glances over the rim
  Of a martini glass
Caress and promise.

No one whispers across a café table anymore.
In the crossword puzzle of life
  In the new millennium,
There is no across
Only
Down.

Heads focus in that direction
  As hands caress a device
  And thumbs feverishly whisper a text message
To the someone sitting across the table
Texting a reply:

U R an idiot!

--Nancy Morley

AIRPORT SATURDAY NIGHT, 7:45 PM

like a hospital waiting room, airport departure wings are full of
small talk and long silences and what lies underneath. I see
parents sitting on either side of me at the gate
philadelphia, back when you could do that kind of thing.
I always protested.
they always insisted.

now I follow my honey blonde college girl around
bradley international terminal, clinging to the
seconds before she succumbs to security,
asking questions that don't matter with urgency.
do you have something to read?
she raises her hand slightly to stop me, blinks affirmatively.

we've already said as much as could be said
considering. she is the age when I started to
know myself. I remember so well I think
she is me. when she lets me into her worries
I remember too well: we share the same nervous system.
I feel her burdens like they are my own.
mostly I am relieved she trusts me again.
I am redeemed after the silent years, the secret
years, the scary years.

north gate now. I let her release me first from
our embrace. our parting words stumble out jaggedly.
whatagreatvisitgoodluckyeahitwasmomwitheverythingimsoproudofyouthank
youcallmewhenyouiwilliwillarrive.
then I watch as she moves forward into the jaws
of the larger world. she doesn't turn back
until the last second, knows I wait for this
final crumb—the one who leaves has all the power—

she raises her hand birdlike and barely smiles without teeth,
but her eyes dance
when I play my part as the pursuing suitor waving with all of me.
then I watch the hem of her trench coat follow her around the corner.

--Nancy Murphy

YEAR OF THE SNAKE

some nights when they sleep
he enters the room
comes between them in the bed
there is space enough,
he slides into the warm sheets
slithers over to her side
wraps around her and gently
presses her skin squeezes
the life from her
threatens her with disaster.

       she thinks this is sexy
       she has no idea.

the snake stays the night wanting
her dreams, she opens her eyes
early morning feels around
for something vaguely
unfinished
the way night stories can be,
but he is gone pulled back
to his own bed
his own woman
her thick honey hair and soft hips
waiting wanting to bear
children, he has
made his choices he has
spoken his vows.

       let's meet for coffee he says
       that cafe in the hills she says
       but they never do.

she rolls onto her side
now listens for the alarm,
when it sings she reaches
her entire body across
the mountain of her man,
she stays there as he
awakens encircles her,
she holds on to him
for dear life.

--Nancy Murphy

ASCENT

The sunset orange fear that burns through me
Is only diminished by the frozen isolation of the seaside cliff,
I ascend the rocks,
Clinging to crackly brine,
Clear blue air fills my lungs with salt,
My parched lips ache as much as my calloused hands,
As I scrabble up the craggily rocks,
Lone gulls fly overhead,
Filling the air with their melancholy cries
So enraptured by the call,
My hands slip,
Tinting the rocks rust red,
I cry out,
Sending the birds in a scatter
I force myself onwards
Attempting to reach the cobalt covered sky,
Glittering like a million tiny diamonds scattered across a
Pool of murky water

--Elliott Negrin

FROST'S END: FIRE IN ICE

Caged in ice, shelved undersea
Lies methane gas.
From what I know of energy
Incontinence, I'll bet on greed.
But if we go with ice uncapped
By Fahrenheit and Centigrade,
And tundra thawing to morass,
It still escapes,
It will be tapped.

--Janet Nippell

HERO

Hi Penelope, Queen of Ithaca
tall, dark haired fairy of my childhood
princess of rebellion and faith.
Did you win your battle against greed and power
and in favor of patience... did you?
Countless years sitting at the loom
weaving and unweaving your web
with a steady beat, a firm pulse
like a moon incessantly waning and waxing
in the sky deep and black
like the ocean where Ulysses is lost.
Since when? You don't know
because you stopped time in the island
with a tight loop, with the nervous twitch
of your hand, your eyes down.

Was he worth it?
When the young lads who reached
for the throne vibrated with arrogance
didn't you ever desire them?
Didn't you feel alone? Was your bed
ever cold or unbearably hot or too wide?
Like the ocean where Ulysses is lost.
Since when you don't know, for you lost
your mind. Were you insane from the start?
A poor speechless woman.
All you knew were uxorial duty
the care of the house and the thread.
You kept quietly in your place.
You've been waiting for your entire life.

Tonight he comes back.
You heard the dog bark because of his smell
a thin blade cutting through scents of sweat

liquor, flowers. Now a cane
hits the pavement of the porch.
Light clicks. They get louder.
And your lips disclose, Queen, my love.
You say nothing. You sing ancient songs.

--Toti O'Brien

GRANDMA FANNY

I belong to you
you give me grandma kisses
your eyes shine, loving
healing me from mama spite
                (or is it mama's bite?)
you're gone. where's my safe place now?

I was the eldest child of Grandma Fanny's favorite son.

She cooked. That's what she did, and what a fantastic cook she was. Her
kosher pickles sizzled when you bit into them. If she made a cake for
company and I came early, she would cut me a piece and serve it later with
Marsha's piece missing. When people asked what happened to the cake, she
would wink at me. Phyllo dough for cherry strudel rolled out over the entire
dining room table was so sheer the pattern of the tablecloth showed through.
I slept on a Murphy-in-a-door bed when I spent the night.

When she was alive, extended family gathered there for holidays. After, no
one would do the work.

She died from breast cancer, her arm and hand swollen huge like a ham hock.
No one ever told me why. Later, I had it, too.

--Marsha Oseas

LEAVES FALLING

leaves fall
over the telephone wires
with soft grace
with no apparent plan
or sense of haste
the yellow ones have the sun
burning in them
nothing urgent makes them
spin downward
in the passing breeze
they have mastered the plan,
the yearly dying
and what telephone lines carry
in scrambled complexity
are nothing to them
they fall in free time
and have no knowledge of the volts
and vexations of man
traveling in milliseconds
through telephone lines
they flit through these
vehicles of force,
insouciant, careless and free
mindless of electricity

--Alice Pero

Originally published in *Poet Lore*, Fall/Winter 2008.

HESITATION

I would cast myself
before danger,
even die,
for wife or child.

might do the same,
without thinking,
for an undetermined few,

but hesitate,
just enough,
for a friend or colleague,
to get us both killed.

--dp (Dalton Perry)

PRAY/PREY

parents
nag
chide
worry
frustrate
smother…
for fear
that demons
haunting them
might turn
to hunt
their children

--Albie Preciado

CORRAL OF THE DEAD

they call it, these twin acres of stones like weary sentries in
cockleburrs and thorns, devils of dust swirling between and among.
Headstones limed and streaked by rain or tilted by spirits on neighbors,
sod crushed by mourning feet. Crude blocks soothed, smoothed
by generations of pilgrim hands who touch names and remember.

Corrals circumscribe what we grant them: bones and flesh dissolving
to dirt, histories gasped in granite and slate, measured meters of coffined
plots—the dead now landowners in perpetuity, this spit of space theirs
to rule, to squat, to prove the dead don't die.

Corrals are circles sans beginnings, with sham promises of
holding precious things intact. We send loved ones
underground tethered by rituals and obligations, spirits and bodies
rent asunder, then plundered further by earth. In sickness and in health, with
death not doing us part, we visit corrals, pull parasite vines from marble,
bring flowers doomed to wilt by noon, pray, and resurrect doubts
about the living and the dead.

Corrals of the dead bind us, wind us so tightly, we never
let go, can never be free. Spirits intoned stay slaves on earth:
named,
        marked,
                beseeched,
                        invoked,
infinitely present in absentia.

--Thelma T. Reyna

Originally published in a prior version in *Spectrum 4: 2016's Top Ten San Gabriel Valley Poets.* (Spectrum Publishing, 2016).
[The title phrase was inspired by Gabriel Garcia Marquez' use of "corral for the dead" in his novella, "Leaf Storm," *Collected Novellas.* (HarperCollins Publishers, 1990). Otherwise, this poem has no connection to Marquez' work.]

BUSTLE

The bustle in a house / The morning after death /
Is solemnest of industries / Enacted upon earth.
--Emily Dickinson, c. 1866

Not death, but the stab is much the same. I strip sheets from beds,
plump denuded pillows in stacks wobbling in my closet once
again, scour toys from under desks and beds, gather books
unto jumbled shelves. Just little rituals to keep hands steady, keep
my lips still in rooms still redolent with my angels' stay.

They left, eyes red, right after dawn, packs turtle-like on fragile
backs, tickets scrunched in pockets stuffed with nana's letters
for the flight. At the curb, their mama's suitcase at our feet, their
lips trembled when she gently pried their arms apart and
vanished them through glass doors hissing shut like guillotines.

At home, I sweep and dust in listless arcs. Broken crayons, stubs
of chalk, Skywalker beaming on the sketchpad by their bed, each
relic talismans of them, each leftover relic swept, kissed, and
tossed gently away, till my house becomes itself again. I fold their
blankets dormant till next winter's trip.

In bed, my body spent from cleaning, from the bustle, from
putting love away till three seasons pass again, from
saying goodbye with eyes dry as stone, to be brave for them,
brave, brave nana, I cocoon myself into forlorn quilts and
let my spirit weep.

--Thelma T. Reyna

NEW

New always attracts: new with or without new-car smells.
New lover, hairdo, new leases on life, and all
the rigmarole that clichés tell us represent *new*.

But old is new again, the old saw says, and news aren't
new when TV spews what the web spat out last night. New
is old when the car drives off the lot.

Habits hogtie us to old. New tattoos twist on shriveled skin
with pixilated saints ancient as myth. Demagogue darlings on stage
strut new Bruno Magli shoes and spout dogma calcified with lies.

Old is new and new is old. Novas blazed eternally yet disappear
in blinks. Wizards cast new spells, and medicine men plumb
ancestors' tales to cure the newborn babe.

New is old and old is new. The stripper dreams of adolescent loves
and haunts new bars across the way. Swollen rivers melt their
Neolithic banks in floods stoked by modernity.

Old new, new old, interwoven, stitched together in waves and
swirls, seemingly seamless, deluding and denuding, tricking us to
think we can pinpoint endings and beginnings.

--Thelma T. Reyna

Originally published in a prior version in *2016 San Gabriel Valley Poetry Calendar.*
(Spectrum Publishing, 2016).

BLACK DOG RISING

He lay next to me
like a wooly guard dog
big black and curly

How long had it been
since I brought him home
alone from that other place

The two storied with a pool
he could jump in anytime
And where that man beat him
So much so, that he cringed
when I put my hand out to pet him
and jumped at footsteps on the sidewalk
that came up behind
in the dim light of evening

And one day the groomer said
What happened to his ear
after he cut his hair short
for that first summer shear

Without the big black curls
to hide the shredded ear
I see the shards of flesh
dangling there like a silent mobile.

Now he doesn't jump at footsteps
or cringe when you try to pet his head
Nowhere in his body is there a tremor
or a hint of dread

Now he watches over me instead
and looks out in the dark
for any furtive movement
that causes him to bark

Then comes and licks me when he knows it's safe
Like a thank you for all the love that made him change
as if he knows love can heal almost anything

--R.S. Rocha

AT BANDELIER

Orange light on the crest of the hill;
so many holes to climb inside.
I ascend to one by ladder
and place my palm
at the entrance to a small cavette,
reach in and touch the cold, rock floor
not daring to completely jump inside,
yet wanting to be present there
connected to the ancient time.

The air in the pines, so clear and still
not even a spirit can hide.
My ancestors walk at Bandelier
on the path of cliff dwellers
snow falls in my hair, drop by drop.
I sense them here
and a wave of knowing, a longing
begins to rise, pulling in me.
I pause underneath a juniper.

Then go; my friends wait in the car.
But I do not want to leave.
There is a shimmering in the trees.
Perhaps the play of sun
on snow drops among the pine,
or the jewelling of a memory.
I cannot tell; but I drink my fill.
The crystalline air inside of me,
my ancestors and I walk on.

--Susan Rogers

SHIAWASE*

White butterfly
air dancer, spirit whisperer
sudden sunlight
caught in a breath.

I ask you to land
on my hand.
Oh irrepressible light
shiawase.

I cannot command
nor anticipate your flight.
Only reach out
to you

near the fluttering flower,
planter of fragrant herbs,
tomato vine
without expectation.

Quiet my heart
as you circle
the colors I have planted
blessing them.

--Susan Rogers

Shiawase: Japanese word for happiness.

CHILDHOOD ADVENTURE STORY

It is always more fun
to do what I am told not to do.
That's why I am here
in the basement climbing up
Mt. Pittsburgh Post-Gazette,
stacks of dailies and Sundays
my father stores in the cellar.
They stand ten to twelve feet high,
uneven enough for toeholds.
Me and Edmund Hillary
climb up the ink-stained summit.
The weather is fine, the sherpas break
camp when unseen disaster strikes:
I slip, scissor-legged, like a wishbone,
one leg in the abyss between the stacks,
the other atop another pile,
my left shoe, the culprit,
dangling like a dripping icicle.
I flash to my death in a dark hole
between piles of Peanuts, recipes
for Spam souffle', Hints from Heloise,
never to be found again because
I'm not supposed to be down here
in the first place. By sheer fear
of what my mother will say,
I hoist myself up to the top
of the waiting stack, slide down
to the hard safety of cool cement,
run up the basement stairs which (of course)
I'm not supposed to do
when I trip and break my wrist
just like mom said I would
and now have to write left-handed like

This...

--Diana Rosen

SNAPSHOT

This is my mother, smiling
Even though she hates to have her picture taken.
She's standing between her two daughters
On the deep grass of her mother's house.

Her golden hair swept into a Grace Kelly chignon
Dressed in navy and white
With matching spectator shoes
Always the classics, she says, they never go out of style.

Here is my sister: poised, posing,
Right foot ahead of the left the way the models stand, she says.
Sis and I wear matching wide-brim hats, Bermuda shorts,
Sleeveless cotton blouses, uniforms of the summer of '58.

It's a happy row of three smiling females:
One proud mother, two teenagers on a day of civility.
Soon the woman who loves us will be dead,
Leaving a space too wide for our arms to embrace.

--Diana Rosen

THE FACE OF THE BOY

Because of these last twenty days
I read *as he practices dying,* not *tying*
and I think how smooth your brow that last night.

I laid my palms on the sides of your face
as if modeling it in clay, traced
the high cheekbones, your perfectly shaped

eyebrows scant as a woman's. I left you
to go to your brother, left without knowing
you'd be gone in four hours, your eyelids

nearly translucent when I said goodbye.

--Cathie Sandstrom

VIGIL

Fragmented on the kitchen sill, a piece
of white granite, fissured at midpoint:

an inverted "W." Running cipher for mountain,
pointy and stretched wide like a child would draw.

Whole when I lifted it off the path, some
small disturbance has caused it to break apart.

Visible as the trail climbs, fold after fold
of mountain, serried planes that echo

the cipher's broad wings. Sun an hour up
casts a deep Manzanita shadow

across ridge-folds; the now familiar symbol
upended, scribbled dialect of stone, shrub and light.

Pattern laddering up, like the twining
helix selecting traits for variance

so that while brothers resemble each other
inexactly, each could carry the same deadly rift.

On both sides of the twisted strands, the marker
for addiction. Father, brother—husband, son.

And you, second son, still standing.

--Cathie Sandstrom

LAZARUS

A soul, dead,
Or so it seemed.
Wake up! Come out!

The cries of the Spirit
Heard, loud and clear,
Begin to permeate.

He moves,
Step by step,
Into the light,

Out of the cave.
Unwrapped to breathe.
Life once again.

--Elsa M. J. Seifert

I LOOK IN THE MIRROR AND SEE

An activist, aging
Passion intact, energy waning,
Everything gets done,
It just takes a little longer.

Priorities, priorities.
What's important, what is not.

Mind, sharp as a tack.
Body sometimes giving out.
A day of many activities
Needs to be followed by a day of rest.

Priorities, priorities.
What's important, what is not.

--Elsa M. J. Seifert

Originally published in *The Courage to Write.* (Falcon Creek Books, 2011).

WINTER

seedcases harden
worms shed skin in rocky soil
I wrap presents for my niece and her sons
silver bows catch low sunlight
scissors slip stabbing
the tender place between thumb and forefinger
my eyes water

The Bluff Trail at *Montana de Oro* invites
otters' mating screech clack of abalone shells
kelp forests just beneath the surface
silver tailed hawk coasting on air currents
aroma of sage and salt spray
my refuge my sanctuary

I do not return the phone call
of the woman who wants to hike with me
The Betrayer
she belittles my work
trumpets her children's awards
changes lanes without warning
she would steal starfish from tide pools

--Nancy Shiffrin

Originally published in the author's *The Vast Unknowing,* (Infinity
Publishing, B&N.com)

BROWNING MUSHROOMS: A LIFE LESSON

Slice fresh mushrooms
Heat oil in skillet
Have patience
Let the flame do the work

--Julia Robinson Shimizu

∼§

BLUEPOOL

I swam in the rain for the first time.
Droplets piercing arms, back, shoulders
nightstars clouded
bluepool pocked with shards of light
I swam

--Julia Robinson Shimizu

YESTERDAY'S ROSES

My arms are full of yesterday's
roses, once carefully placed in a
finely etched glass vase,
now dried and faded
from the sun's rays peeking
through the patio door
during these unseasonably
warm winter days.

Before the sun falls below our
beloved Verdugo Mountains,
I remove what remains from
the vase, recalling the pleasure
of such a gift from him who
loves to tend the garden
with hands and heart familiar
with the soil in all seasons –

These hands I love.

--Dorothy Skiles

SOULS SPEAK

There was a knowing before…

When my brother and I
were in the womb
close to our mother's heart.
He entered the world first
and I soon followed.
He didn't stay,
and I was to struggle
those first few months.
Death broke the bond,
a bond as strong as
the umbilical cords
that anchored us
to our mother.
For years, I felt the yearning
to be connected again.
It wasn't until my own twins
were born that I understood…

Souls speak long before
the mind can remember,
the heart can understand.

--Dorothy Skiles

172

VICTORIA CAN KEEP HER SECRETS, I'M GONNA SUPPORT MYSELF

Supporting myself
Seemed much harder than
Supporting someone else

Often
I felt like my first training bra
Small cotton triangles
Meant to cover up
Budding breasts
Made to feel older
More substantial
As I blossomed into puberty

I then felt more
Like a padded
Push-up Miracle bra
It looks full
With or without the boob
On or off
Seems to make no difference
In it's form or shape
Its rigid support structure built in
Uncaring about what they held up

I have outgrown the training bras
The training wheels
The façade of support
Or store bought miracles

I now know
That I can support myself
Bra or no bra
That my cup can runneth over

Without looking tacky
Causing pain, restricting my breath
Or looking like someone else
In the dark

Because it is what's inside
That counts

--Becky Skoglund

THE SLIDE

"One must imagine Sisyphus happy."
--Albert Camus

Angled upward, lean into it,
Keds hard-pressed, determined
against the funhouse mirror.
It reflects only the blur
of your wincing smile.

Climb
clench-fisted,
grab handfuls of glaring heat,
sneakers jammed into right angles
traveling acutely toward the nearest star.

One grasp away
from your goal,
feel the tread
of your brother's right shoe
against your forehead.
Smell the new rubber, old gum.
He took the easy way up.

Together you squeak
squeal
lurch
lunge
glide glide
then fall
into a knotted heap,
his body crushing yours into the sand.

Grit clings to the sweat
of arms pumping,
grinds against the soles

of feet running,
of hands grabbing
hold of steel soaring
once more into the sun.

--David Slavin

BROADWELL DRY LAKE

My elbows rest on the surface of the water.
Under the glare of the sun, the water trembles
my ears resonate with the silence.

A crow circles in the lake of the sky.
I hear a caw, an echo of a caw
as it settles in a withered cottonwood.

The blue of the water nurses
a necklace of turquoise apertures
fingered by dead branches.

A splash of orange hovers
above, below the horizon;
an old cinder cone

and its reflection
in this ancient sea.
It is autumn in the desert.

A dune rises to eclipse the sun
as I rise and brush the dust
from the folds of my shirt.

I taste desert brine,
breathe in salt spray;
the water has receded.

And now Venus is revealed
as she wades naked, radiant
into the black pool of a night sky.

--David Slavin

NEW YEAR'S EVE

A woman made tipsy by the streetlights
begins a slow waltz with a pack of cigarettes,
lets go the string that tethers the moon.

Unmoored, it floats
into the dark sea above LAX
trafficked by ships with firelit galleys.
I can hear the pulling of the oars.

The moon is trapped in telephone wires.
It glows orange, now yellow,
bleeds out, feeds the murmurs,
the ecstatic laughter
traveling the lines.

It grows pale, deflates,
slips free of the cables
while the woman takes deep drags
the tobacco, and her eyes, burning bright.

--David Slavin

THUMBING THROUGH THE NIGHT

Turning
on —no, pressing --
the device beside
the bed, its face
lights up, relieving itself
of the night's missives
which you check
hoping the light
won't wake
the one on the other
side: the night's drama

is you, unable
to resist, shamefaced
at your need
to know, more
humiliating than being
found with your hand
on a private part -- no, more so

because this need is just
as urgent
and shouldn't be.
To know should also go
to sleep and wake with you, then
and only then
to render its latest,
allowing you a morning
surge of power
as you swipe
away opportunities.

But it's the middle
of the night
and the screen is glowing

although, like you, the battery
is low, but it's the middle
of the night
and the screen is glowing
although, like you,
the battery is low, perhaps a few
minutes left
to read, you are
running down, you are being
given a message
you cannot delete.

--Janet Sternburg

ABSORPTION

To forgive my body
is to love the young, their long
fresh lashes, their pert laps,
their leanings toward each other,
absorbed (and not), desiring
(and not)

these moats
of youth, and my
napkin slipping off my angled
aging knees, I am

utterly absorbed in this:
her elbows on the table, hands
clasped at her cheek, her golden
cowl

he wipes her mouth, slides
the napkin across her lips

and mine
drops to the floor: am I
absorbed in my wish to be
them? Doesn't matter. It is
matter.

--Janet Sternburg

OPEN CITY

only time ever I had
                    Mogen David wine

    news stand @ Echo Park Avenue
                    says *Open City* not
                            published any more
                            out of business shut down

                                        Bukowski serialized

no more
        notes of a dirty old man
                        I looked forward to it every week
                                            I had no other life
    I go to Melrose 'n Heliotrope office
            where it's demise
                            is being celebrated
                                    mourned

    there's nothing for me to do
                        just no more
                                notes

        but accept the offer of Mogen David

                                    and that's all there was to it

--Robert Stewart

CALIFORNICATIN'

Eat breakfast of cream cheese spread on bagel,
not biscuits, bacon and scrambled eggs
and drink cup of kona, not Maxwell House coffee

Say, boy, ain't you gittin' too big for your britches?

Crew cut gone, now have a mustache and beard
Wear jeans and sandal
not polyester and wing tips

Say, boy, ain't you gittin' too big for your britches?

Reading Dostoevsky, Kafka and Joyce
Think that I shall never see
a more philistine poem than "Trees."

Say, boy, ain't you gittin' too big for your britches?

Can't stomach the reader's Digest no more
Stopped buying used cars from Tricky Dick
Hell, Jimmy Carter's too far right for me!

Say, boy, ain't you gittin' too big for your britches?

Dig the sounds of Billie, Miles and Trane
but unswayed by Hank's honky tonk twang
or the teary love songs of Patsy Cline

Say, boy, ain't you gittin' too big for your britches?

Cheer depressing foreign flicks with English subtitles:
jeer macho John Wayne, hokey Jimmy Stewart
and upbeat Doris Day movies

Say, boy, ain't you gittin' too big for your britches?

Break down in California license plated Dodge in parkin' lot
of Oklahoma rest home before gittin' out for what'll
probably be the last time I'll ever see my grandma alive

Hey, man, looks like you lost a little weight!

--Carl Stilwell

I HAVE

patio view of evening purple clouds passing over Colorado
Blvd 99¢ store on way to Pasadena Community College where
my two sons, Luke and Mark, along with their mother, Cheryl,
began their university education

a little over 100 neighbors in the condominium where I live
a state teacher's retirement pension allotting me enough each
month to pay Homeowners Associate fees and purchase at Trader Joe's
free range eggs, cans of refried beans, corn tortillas, green, red and
jalapeño peppers for my *huevos a la Mexicaño* breakfast

the Catalina Branch of the Pasadena Public Library
where Kingfisher drives me in his Cube to poetry workshops, critiques
and readings every Saturday afternoon and the honor of having
my poems published alongside those of a galaxy of poets
in the Altadena Poetry Review, Lummox and Spectrum

a Senior citizen Metro card where for 50¢ a day
I can travel by Gold, Red and Expo lines to Santa Monica where
upon the city pier, I can watch on beach brown-bearded father
hold in a waist high ocean from whence all life emerged
redheaded son looking like my Mark
or to downtown Citibank near Pershing Park where protectors
with WATER IS LIFE and YOU CAN'T DRINK OIL signs protest
corporate investment in the North Dakota Access Pipeline

I have also
a second-floor balcony view where I can see
along transverse San Gabriel Mountain range when looking right
morning magenta clouds sailing west from African motherland
where journey of humans began some 150,000 years ago
and looking north to Mount Wilson summit their eastern pilgrimage
toward a cherry tree near Hiroshima where
over cremated remains of firstborn, Luke, its blossoms
will fall in the spring

--Carl Stilwell

PREFACE TO A HAIKU

Maiden voyage to Santa Monica on Metro Expo line
Get on at Metro 7th St
Standing room only
Compassionate commuter offers me his seat
Rail ride almost as bumpy as bus one to same city
Forever and ever like rolling over slow tide
Wonder if it's worth it
But after nearly two hours on rail from Pasadena
and I step out under blue skies with white flowing clouds
while inhaling salty ocean breeze
as I walk to Santa Monica pier,
there's no doubt it was

Walk over rugged pier planks to Coffee Bean
Order coffee with blueberry muffin and take to outdoor table
Read Luke's poem about how his wife, Masami, as a child of
Hiroshima Prefecture, was shipped out to the Peace Park every
year along with her class to go through the Museum there
It was a non-stop tour of the horrors that began on August 6, 1945
with plenty of gruesome photos and exhibits
She couldn't take it and kept her eyes down the whole time
Every year after, she found some kind of excuse to miss that trip
I had never cried reading this poem previously
but on picture postcard day over Southern California shore I cry
for—
Massami's loss of innocence before unconscionable evil and
suffering,
the loss of my firstborn at 47 from rectal cancer
and the human sacrifice of over 140,000 in Hiroshima
and 70,000 in Nagasaki to the hellfire god of nuclear war
Then across wharf
from man of Asian Indian descent between
white-blue speckled sky and sandy earth
comes to me
sitar music
Pulling laptop from backpack
I begin to write—

To sitar beat from
Santa Monica Pier
waves dance to beach

--Carl Stilwell

THE PHOTOGRAPHER

I saw you like artwork
the features of your face all in
perfect balance like landscape
ridges of your brows
canyons of your eyes
and the lining of red bristle stalking
your cheeks and jawline

I saw you in completion
between us, some chemistry
the noted composition
of my streaming half notes captured
by your camera
as you dictated my body
to bask like anemone
over rocky edges of Malibu

then, even the long car ride home
couldn't explain the tightness in my stomach
as I laughed or the fold of your knees before, as we
sat against the shore, the universe of stars, our backdrop
I am the painter, you are the spectrum and
this is the momentary lapse of judgment

You said: "we are born from the ashes of stars"
I shake my head, with a crashing smile
the last hour becomes plastic
the last hour is divided
and we are separated through
a lense

--Sachi Terry

ANATOMY OF YOUR SPACE

When twelve o'clock draws me down
Like the flat part of a joke, the credits
Of the last tv addiction
I taste the space you left wide open
The cool air in San Francisco must be warm
With your space

When beautiful things go missing:
The character in my voice
The steam from my favorite dish
I try to relocate your laughter
The precise inflection of your voice
Delivering a signature phrase

It's coming on 2 a.m. and the Christmas lights have
Been unplugged, the flame in the candle is gone
The book is falling in my lap, and the last sip
Of wine has started to dry out around
The edges

Yet my insides are flapping around like
Wings scraping against caging, trying
To feather out some needed remnant
Of my other half-sister
Carrying a toss of shared chromosomes
My swelling heart is digging out an old
Grave of yours with
My own nostalgia
The minimalist is fighting the battle of savor, I'm convinced
There is space here belonging to you

--Sachi Terry

MY GREAT-GRANDPARENTS
AND THE BURKINI BAN

--After "Debate over 'burkini' bans heats up further in France"
(L.A. Times, 8/19/16)

Zipporah. She is covered from head to toe
with an apron and layers of cloth. *There is*
the idea that...women are immodest, impure,
that they should therefore be completely

covered. Wool scarves swirl around her
hidden neck in the black and white photo.
A headscarf, a "tichel," hides every strand
of great-grandmother's wig. [This] *is not*

compatible with the values of France and
the Republic. Zipporah—bird in Hebrew.
She flew from Russia to a brownstone
in Baltimore. She sits on a stoop, even her

hands are invisible; we see only her withered
face. She is over a hundred. *I issued this order...*
to ensure the safety of my city...I am only
prohibiting a uniform that is the symbol

of Islamist extremism. Zipporah—a bird who
flew away before I was born. She sits next
to my great-grandfather in the black and white
photo. Hasidic white beard, yarmulke

between him and his God. *It is the soul*
of France that is in question...France does not
hide half of its population under the...odious
pretext that the other half would be afraid

190

of temptation. An oversized wool suit envelops
his body and his fringes. In the 32mm film,
he blesses my mother and her sisters. His body
rocks. Back and forth, back and forth. He recites

prayer. Pious great-grandfather who gave me
my name. *The beaches, like any public space,
must be preserved from religious demands.* My
great-grandparents—covered in fabric and faith.

--Judith Terzi

Italics are direct quotes from the Prime Minister, the Minister for women's rights, and the
Mayor of Cannes. First appeared in a different version in *The New Verse News*, 8/22/16.

TO A YOUNG PROSPECTOR

You've staked your claim,
named it "Home Run,"
and bought all your mining tools,
your dredge, sluice, and pan.
Your prospects look good
to keep what you find.
El oro es tuyos, all yours.

You camp among the tall timbers,
near a stream. Even spot bears
your mother warned you against.
Los osos son peligrosos, dangerous!
But you're on your way to riches.
You'll disturb the surface, then the universe
in search of glorious glints.

Before you strike out, consider this:
Where is the gold country?
I say it's within reach,
in the wild cove
del corazón, your heart.

--Mary Langer Thompson

MALEVOLENCE

Malware
found me
one prolific night.
Stole my words,
my voice,
my malapropisms,
illiterating them from memory
yet holding them for ransom,
for real.

Pay in bit coins
the red pop-up page demanded,
by a certain date
after which the price will rise.

I examine my maladjusted bank account
and draw my optical conclusion:

Byte me!

--Mary Langer Thompson

DERAILED
Orange County, California, 1889

May I have this dance, Miss Modesta Avila?
asked Fernando from Santa Ana.
I agreed, laughing. This was my day.
I had bested the railroad.

They laid tracks so close to my front door
I couldn't sleep, my chickens eggless.
I stood between those rails in my home-made dress,
hammered a fencepost on either side
then strung my laundry, still wet
across the tracks.
I added a sign:
This land belongs to me!

An agent stripped my damp clothes off the line.
The police waited for me, until after the party,
arrested me near the church as I walked home.
Fernando watched helplessly with a ring in his pocket.

I've served almost three years here in San Quentin.
I would be released
if not for this fever I'm not going to beat.

I've already heard my obituary will say
I was a favorite of those Santa Ana boys.
I hear the train's whistle every night.

--Mary Langer Thompson

KAZAKHSTAN, 1936

Expelled, deported, one day to pack.
Homes, orchard, farms, animals —
all left behind.

It was not fair. Why did they hate us?
Why did they lie?
They told us: "There are no winters in hot Kazakhstan."
They told us: "You do not need warm clothes in hot Kazakhstan."
They told us: "There is no salt in hot Kazakhstan."

We brought the wrong things.

My friends were taken up north,
to a small village.
Pasiolki, we used to call them.
The Kazakhs were kind.
They helped them out, gave them
wool, sheepskin, old gloves.

We had to build our huts
in a wide-open steppe.
Dig wells for water.
Make bricks of mud.
Dry bricks in the fire.
We did not have wood
for the fire.
There were no trees
to stop the sharp spikes
of wind from piercing our bodies,
to keep sand from hurting our eyes.

Old folks and babies died first.
We persevered. We worked hard.

Only the evenings with howling winds.
Only the night skies with different stars.

Only the foreign sounds seeping into our mouths,
lilting in melodies of a new language —

Our Polish language,
frozen in Kazakhstan.

--Maja Trochimczyk

UNDER AFRICAN SKY
For painter Julian Stanczak

— amber and coral —
— ruby and carnelian —

He looks at the brightness of the African sky.
The blazing sunset above the plains of Uganda
His eyes follow the pattern of light and shadow
on the savanna's tall grass. Dark lines cut
into light on the flanks of a zebra —
he thinks of a donkey back home,
transformed by the extravagant, geometric
boldness of stripes, shining bright —

blinding his eyes, used to Siberian darkness
in dim interiors of musty prison huts —
he admires the play of gold and bronze inside
the tiger's eye — a stone his teacher gave him
for protection and good luck. How it shifts
with each turn, different, yet the same —
lines upon lines of light.

The richness stays under his eyelids
as he twists and turns the tiger's eye
in his one good hand, left — while the other,
a useless appendage, hangs limply
since that beating in a Soviet prison camp.
Shattered, like his dream of music,
the honey-rich tones of his cello.

He finds a different-flavored honey
in the richness of African sunsets,
the stripes of the tiger's eye.

He captures the undulating lines
and blazing hues on majestic canvas,
moving in the rhythm of wild planes
out of Africa, into fame.

— amber and topaz —
— gold, bronze, and light —
— so much light —

--Maja Trochimczyk

Originally published in *The Rainy Bread. Poems from Exile.*
(Moonrise Press, 2016).

FEMALE IDOL FROM THE CYCLADIC ISLANDS

I am tired of standing naked here
Thirty hundred years now with no break.
Let me lie in the arms of higher power (s)
Protected, breathing moist baby breaths.
Not perched on this stark cold stone marble plaque
Molded into your form and given a name.
They look at me drunk, amused and sometimes I'm forgotten.
Once this old woman from Calcutta passed me
And through a tube, asked what would it feel like?
To be stripped? Striped? Spotted?
Please cover up my rock chassis and let me turn in my key.
Looking into nothing is not good for me anymore.
There is no independence, no critique and no worship.

--Claudine Voznick

VIGNETTES OF EDWARDS AIR FORCE BASE

Flying high above the Mojave Desert,
the sun's rays ricochet off a silver
winged jet, which soars faster than speed of sound.
The "boom" created from breaking the sound
barrier shakes the land like an earthquake
and sends long eared jack rabbits for cover.

As tumbleweeds drift along with the wind,
ruins of a ranch hidden from view tell
past stories of a lively place pilots
used to visit. Charred foundations whisper
airmen's hushed dreams of aircraft thought
to be science fiction, but have since become real.

--Lori Wall-Holloway

Originally published in *Phantom Seed 2,* (2008).

A BLOODY MARY IN THE KIBITZ ROOM

And then there are the hunched minor martyrs,
bloodless miseries moaning and shaking to Piaf
and other near-love disasters in the cold cadaver
gray of this boom town bar, this last human trough.

The remains of a woman steeped in White Linen
and warm whiskeys rot next to me, hissing in
one rheumatic breath, *I once danced for a senator –*
followed with convent severity, *I was only 24.*

Somewhere in the city, a beaten cat stiffly
makes its way down an alley while I stir my
Bloody with a fork and rock to the airless rhythm
of this sick soul's chewed ice, her recycled hymn.

       Something is unraveling, loosening in my head –
       Did you hear me, blonde thing? A senator, I said!

--Jennifer Welsh

SLIME

Not long after he had pranced back to his wife, the runner-up paces in a storm, *stupid, stupid, stupid*, where she spies the infant snail, also stupid, and so new it hasn't yet sprouted its armor, no bigger than a toddler's pinky, spongy and meaty, raindrops plopping like pewter upon its whisker-propped eyes. *Oh dear*, muses our heroine, *musn't let it be crushed!* Squatting, she encourages the little oozer onto a damp leaf with quick taps to the rump. But it balls up, confused, *why, why, why*? And there the pair stay, marooned, hunched in the wet wind, goners.

--Jennifer Welsh

WIDOWER

Green, both of them, man and flat
of thyme, wet, fresh, pensive they sat

together, the pick chipping hollows
in the stiff, stubborn stone soil, blows

falling quickly, inexpert and earnest,
the sun moseying toward the west.

I've dug their graves he thinks, prying
the seedlings apart, cradling, lowering

them like injured birds into the curt
toothless mouths gaping in the dirt,

covering and patting the pebbles around
their cowed stems, their burial mound.

He'll never be the gardener she was –
he's forgotten the hat, the hope, the gloves.

--Jennifer Welsh

IN THE TIME BEFORE PLANETARY RELATIONS

In the old days, humans used to
engage in something they called war.
A war was when two or more groups
went to work killing each other
and destroying one another's
land and creations.

All the different groups
had their own territories
and they'd disagree over where
the boundaries were and who
was crossing over and who
had rights to the resources,
and they'd "settle"
their disagreements
by blowing things up
and killing people.

Sometimes they'd pretend they were fighting
over moral issues, and sometimes they'd fight
over whether others were ready or able to fight.
Really.

They would all build weapons
and then they would start wars
over the fact that others had weapons
or even just because they were afraid
that others had weapons,
whether they did or not.

Honestly. They did this.

But that was before.
That was in the age of...
well, we haven't exactly

named that age,
but that was
before.

--Mari Werner

BIRD'S EYE
For Toti O'Brien

my bird's eye view
the world is wind
wing a brush
canvas blue and roses
paint the ground pink

her open book

how she disappeared --naked into the night. Her jewel-like sighs
took shape as opal, pink sapphire, stardust. The text of her song
preserved in mono-prints, her solo arias, arms outstretched in jubilation.

all she could say
deciphered breath on glass
clouds falling
her white lace veil
her fern-like smile

she was she angel's mother
taught her everything she knows
blue she said
I'll be that and you be
all the other colors

--Kath Abela Wilson

These verses were inspired by artwork by Toti O'Brien: *For Descanso #3, Scattering the Maze*; "Sonetto in Morte di Madonna" and "She Angel." Displayed in the show, "Secret Essence in our Living Room Gallery," Autumn, 2016.

RESERVOIR

"Daddy, he said, why do the birds sit on the water?" All of us in the car were suddenly quiet. 1954 Chevy, going by the reservoir, white gulls on blue. He was my little brother and it was his first sentence. I don't remember the answer.

oldest boy
when dad left
the family
he felt the weight
of keeping it all afloat

--Kath Abela Wilson

SOLITUDE
For Mark

I look up to see the mountain
The snow comes down upon my porch in winter.
Looking at clouds while flakes of white fall upon the thatch of my
Cottage
Yet…
I wish to be THERE – part of the clouds, the sky
Ceiling of my world.
Among flakes of water, once not snow, but clouds.
My face is warm now…
The sun has come; it is spring.

--John L. Wiltshire

GOD'S BREATH

For Brian Thorpe

The place where I grew up is gone now, winds blew in from the sea.
Town's people said it was God's breath;
I don't really know, sure sounded nice though.

I visited from time to time after I had left, But not anymore.
The breeze still comes in after summer.
Now I know God's breath is still there, but the wind that swept
Childhood left me rustling leaves of other saplings now.

The scents of life are gone too, there in that place.
God still breathes; I am and am not;
Forgotten, lost in a summer breeze.

Bridges join a place like that with another.
I crossed them seeking new adventures when I was still there,
Breathing in, breathing out. Summer Saplings get a kind of strength those
Zephyrs' of God bring to them.

Time passes, as determined, and we fly on them,
Across the bridges that join a place with another.
Structure still exists, within the town,
But that other time has passed,
Crossing one bridge or another to that place;
God's voice, at times ceases to be.

--John L. Wiltshire

SHADY LADY

black as midnight without a moon
she races around from room to room

after prey she cannot see
catches it and brings it to me

is it some woodland creature
or is it in her mind a feature

no it is a catnip toy she brings
she drops it at my feet and starts to sing

well she doesn't sing, meow or purr
she squeaks, settles and cleans her fur

black as midnight without a moon
shady lady leaves the room

--Joe Witt

UP PERISCOPE

Enemy sighted. Load torpedoes.
Fire 1, fire 2, fire 3, fire 4.
Destroyer coming. Down periscope.
OOGAOOGA. DIVE DIVE DIVE.
Run silent run deep.

"Lunch" my mother calls.
Reluctantly we climb out of our sub
Two large wooden crates, one on top the other.

White star, blue background, in our window.
Redacted letters from my brother
Somewhere at sea.

Gilbert, my brother-in-law, a paratrooper
A POW in Germany.
Donny and Dale, cousins, officers in the corps
Semper Fi. Semper Fi.

Rock grenades, guns made from wood.
We charge the enemy.

Dinner time.

Huddled around the radio.
President's Fire Side Talk.
Then Gabriel Heater
"Ahh, there's good news tonight".

Up periscope!

--Joe Witt

Originally published in *Spectrum* 6, August 2016.

PARROTS

parrots fly above
furiously flapping wings
I too flap fiercely
watching then speeding away
while I remain still in place

--Roz Witt

CAT GAMES

a perfect stillness
eyes are locked, a tail twitches
the black one pounces
twisting clutching the game is on
our bed is an arena

--Roz Witt

UNSPOKEN

the elephant watched
guests sipped coffee and ate cake
chatting and chewing
feet shuffled and eyes shifted
none mentioned the pachyderm

--Roz Witt

HALF ANSWERED

high-strung
weekend anglers
cast flies
adrift with slack
far from the bottom line

seaside stones
worn smooth
by restless waves
settling for questions
half answered

young doe
strolls gracefully by
one glassy eye
reflecting us
looking at her

strapped in
the backseat
babbling directions
only a mother
can decipher

--J.K. Won

NEWBORN

spring in the air
one bluebird feeds another
beak to beak

smiling back
grannies take turns
making clown faces

lobby elevator doors
open and close
changing her baby's diaper

snack rack
toddler reaching for one
beyond her grasp

speeding ahead
on her tricycle
daddy's racing heart

not yet green
a praying mantis explores
my hand instead

--J.K. Won

READINESS IS ALL

right on schedule
eclipse of the moon
what's left to chance?
thank our clockwork stars
then softly knock wood

for love he moved
from flop house
to decent digs
spring garden beds
tease the tiller to toil

Oscar the cat
finds solace in patients
about to expire
terminal to terminal
looking to hitch a ride home

hummingbird
for a moment
we see eye to eye
an inkling of who we are
beyond our kind

burial or cremation
what matter
it's all creation
the rest
is for good

--J.K. Won

TUOL SLENG*

When the power went
it was eight at night.
The fan whirred to a halt.
Churned air settled thick
on my skin, hair and cotton clinging.
There had been rain for five days,
falling in sheets, rapping at the window,
scattering the hawkers, the *motos*,
the men sprawled in their *tuktuks*.
On the kitchen counter, ants
flecked the rambutan plucked
from a wet market stall,
days shy of ripe.

I live behind the Genocide Museum. I wrote home.
It sounds grimmer than it is.

It wasn't the spattered tiles
that got to me most,
or the whites of eyes captured
on camera, the metal beds
on which bodies were strung—but the thought—
of each prisoner's last glimpse
of sun, ruptured, through the shutters
and perforated walls
before the blindfolds, the transport,
fifteen kilometers to *Choeung Ek*,
the Killing Fields, where speakers hung
from The Magic Tree** blaring:

Children, do not forget the fresh blood of our soldiers and
Children, forever remember the revolution!

Now, darkness. New sounds audible,
without the percussive rain and hum of motors:

ceramic on tin, the neighbors' dinner utensils
set to rest. The patter of hands on smooth surfaces,
the collective search for something
to light. In the alley, children with candles, laughing,
thankful for the brief interruption.

--Annette Wong

---

*Tuol Sleng, also known as Security Prison (S-21), was a former high school in Phnom Penh,
Cambodia, which the Khmer Rouge turned into an execution center. Prisoners who were not
killed at S-21 were transported to the Killing Fields for execution. It is now a Genocide
Museum.
**The Magic Tree is a tree in the *Choeung Ek* killing fields upon which the Khmer Rouge strung
loudspeakers that played propaganda and music as victims were being executed.

CALLIGRAPHY

When I learned to write,
my mother began with the elements:

Earth   土
and fire   火
water   水
and wood 木.

Then,
the sky   天,
its sun   日
and moon 月,
clouds   云,
and rain   雨.

Brush to black ink, our hands
traversing the smooth page.

This is how language begins,
with the earth, a mother's voice,
a guiding hand, painting
the world in bold strokes.

--Annette Wong

LAST BREATH

A baby's breath
Makes time disappear
Spring is full of surprises
Summer's tall grasses
The Autumn breeze
Fills me with longing
Knowing soon
The colors will die
Mother takes her last breath
I think it's winter
Time also dies

--Helen Yagake

GLIMPSE

I caught a glimpse of myself
In the glass
Of the patio door
My hair is gray
The glasses unbecoming
The t-shirt is faded
And "holy"
The roses planted years ago
Twirl toward heaven
My yellow lab snores softly
Between me and the reflection
I look happy

--Helen Yagake

SOCKS ASUNDER

Socks asunder.
How could so many go missing?
Now you see them
Now you don't!

My "gold toe' black sock
Is longing for its mate.
In the meantime,
It lies alone
Among happy pairs.

A metaphor, you might think
For my life.
Not so.....
I'm really talking about
Those darn socks
Or is it
Those socks I darn.

In any case,
If you've a solution
For that age old
Problem:
"How to keep
mates together"
Even better,
"How to keep mating,"
Sock it to me!

--Sharon Yofan

UNTAMED

Autumn
Cleaves
To hillsides
Ambers, russets, maroons
Nature's bounty

Inside the symphony of color
Piercing voices
Rehashing
Personal dramas
Messy, angry, chaotic
Flying words

Imperfect humans
In the midst
Of nature's perfection
Mystics say
Let it go
Both beauty and
Beastly

I say
Forget language
Become
More like trees
Alive
In their treeness
Clothed in brilliance
One moment
Naked the next
    Rooted
    Nevertheless

--Sharon Yofan

AUTHOR BIOGRAPHIES

VIBIANA APARICIO-CHAMBERLIN
Vibiana Aparicio-Chamberlin's book, *MI AMOR, A Memoir,* was awarded three prizes by the International Book Awards and won first Prize for Memoir of the Year by the Book Publishers of Southern California. Vibiana won The Southwest Museum's Poetry prize for her sonnet, "Mexican of America." Her award-winning poetry appears in numerous journals. Vibiana recently won a Fellowship from Antioch University to earn an MFA in Creative Nonfiction. She has lived in Pasadena since 1965 and enjoys cooking and painting with her grandchildren, Ava and Gillian, who live in Altadena.

MARIA A. ARANA
Maria A. Arana is a teacher, writer, and poet. Her work has appeared in *Spectrum, vox poetica*, the *Altadena Poetry Review, Poetic Diversity* and others. She was listed as a "Top 10 San Gabriel Valley Poet 2016" by Spectrum Publications. You can learn more about Maria's writings at https://rainingvoices.blogspot.com and https://twitter.com/m_a_Arana

RICHARD ASH
Originally from the DC/Maryland area, Richard Ash has been an Altadena resident for nearly 20 years. He is primarily a songwriter and has had songs recorded by Bobby Womack and Stevie Woods, among others. Writing songs of all genres is his passion, with some songs that are also poems.

SUSAN AUERBACH
Susan Auerbach is a professor of education who has lived in Altadena/Pasadena for 30 years, and is inspired by the beauty of the local mountains. She began writing poetry only recently, after a lifetime of writing in prose. She blogs at Walking the Mourner's Path After a Child's Suicide and is working on a book based on the blog. She is delighted to have this first opportunity to publish a poem.

BETH BAIRD
Beth Baird enjoys spoken word, theater, and music. She has written more than 30 songs which were performed by her former band, Modern Society. Beth loves to write comedic pieces as well as serious works. She has read on the Arroyo Channel Show, *Spending a Little Time with Poetry.* Her love of travel, people, and visual beauty influences her writing.

KATHEE HENNIGAN BAUTISTA

Kathee Hennigan Bautista has lived in the shadows of the San Gabriel Mountains most of her life. She began writing poetry as a child. She taught children with special needs for many years and is the mother of 3 young adults. Dr. Bautista is currently an assistant professor at Azusa Pacific University. During her busy years as a mother and teacher she forgot that she was a poet. She was reminded of this fact at a reunion of friends. Believing that poetry is not just what you write but what you are, she is returning to the practice of writing.

JACK G. BOWMAN

Jack G. Bowman was born to a working class family in southwestern Ohio, but soon moved to southern California. He graduated from California State Polytechnic in 1986 with a BA in Behavioral Science. He graduated from Pacific Oaks College with an MA in Marriage, Family and Child Counseling in 1997. He was nominated for a Pushcart Prize in the 2016 *APR*. Jack is a licensed psychotherapist. Reflections on his work and his life can be found in his 14 books of poetry on Amazon.com and at http://www.thebookpatch.com.

NORMA JEAN BURKS

Norma Jean Burks, 88 years old, originally from Muncie Indiana, and a previous Altadena resident, now resides in Pasadena. She enjoys reading, singing, going to movies, and writing poetry. Although her family did not have much money, they always had books. She has many happy memories of her youth sitting on the floor with a book by her favorite poet, Paul Lawrence Dunbar.

TIM CALLAHAN

Tim Callahan is an artist who worked for many years in the animation industry. He is also a published author and regularly contributes articles to *Skeptic Magazine*. He lives with his wife, Bonnie, in the foothills of Altadena on the edge of the Angeles National Forest and often hikes the Sunset Ridge Trail. He didn't begin to write poetry in earnest until he was in his middle sixties. Tim was nominated for a Pushcart Prize in 2015. He has also served on the Anthology's Selection Committee during 2015–2017.

DON KINGFISHER CAMPBELL

Don Kingfisher Campbell holds an MFA in Creative Writing from Antioch University and has taught Writers Seminar at Occidental College Upward Bound for 32 years. He has been a coach and judge for Poetry

Out Loud, a performing poet/teacher for Red Hen Press Youth Writing Workshops, and a Los Angeles Area Coordinator and Board Member of California Poets in The Schools. Additionally, he has served as poetry editor of the *Angel City Review*, publisher of *Spectrum* and the *San Gabriel Valley Poetry Quarterly,* leader of the Emerging Urban Poets writing and Deep Critique workshops, organizer of the San Gabriel Valley Poetry Festival, and host of the Saturday Afternoon Poetry reading series in Pasadena. His website is: http://dkc1031.blogspot.com

GLORIANA CASEY
Like Walt Whitman, Gloriana has had a plethora of jobs and experiences: ice skater with the Ice Follies; graduate of California State University East Bay with a teaching credential and theatre degree; US Office of Ed. Grant for Creative Dramatics in the Fargo Public Schools; dinner theatre actress; SAG/AFTRA member; copywriter; TV arts reviewer; and tutor. For 5 years, she was a poet with the *Altadena Blog* and the *Altadena Point*. Her ambitions in life have been to follow Frost's "The Road Not Taken" while chasing after Dr. Seuss, and going "On Beyond Zebra."

PEGGY CASTRO
Peggy Castro writes blank verse, haiku and tanka and has been published in numerous journals. She gets great satisfaction in taking photos on her phone and posting them to Facebook with either a tanka or a haiku, particularly at the several gardens where she spends her free time. She works with the homeless as a peer partner and lives with her oldest daughter and son-in-law. Her youngest daughter and five children live in Seattle, Washington. All of this, along with poetry, enrich her life enormously.

JACKIE CHOU
Jackie Chou studied Creative Writing at USC. She writes poetry in an attempt to construct meaning out of everyday experiences, to defy ordinary perceptions, and as an alternative to "ranting" to friends on Facebook. She attends writing workshops and has been published locally. She was listed as a "Top 10 San Gabriel Valley Poet 2016" by Spectrum Publications.

MARSHA CIFARELLI
Marsha Cifarelli was born in Los Angeles in August, 1945. Her mother was holding her when bombs fell on Hiroshima and Nagasaki. She has lived here in LA all of her life, and developed a love of language by raising children and teaching populations with limited English skills, such as

immigrants and students with disabilities. All these experiences honed her ability to say much with little and to communicate a full spectrum of emotions.

STEPHEN COLLEY
Stephen Colley is a retired software engineer who has resided in Altadena for 24 years. He has written and performed classical music, including soprano-and-piano settings of 15 Robert Frost poems. He has also written three screenplays and is a practicing poetaster, who is especially fond of sonnets and triple-limericks.

BEVERLY M. COLLINS
Originally from New Jersey, Beverly M. Collins is the author of the books, *Quiet Observations* and *Mud in Magic* (Moonrise Press). She was one of three 2012 winners of California State Poetry Society's yearly competition. Nominated for the 2015 Independent Best American Poetry Award and the Pushcart Prize, her work appears in *Rubicon: Words & Art Inspired by Oscar Wilde's DeProfundis, Poetry Speaks! A Year of Great Poems and Poets* calendar (Sourcebooks Inc.), *San Gabriel Valley Poetry Quarterly*, *California Quarterly*, the *Altadena Poetry Review 2015 & 2016,* among others.

DEVO CUTLER-RUBENSTEIN
Devorah ("Devo") Cutler-Rubenstein's passion for storytelling and art brought her to Cal Arts where she earned her BFA in Film/Art. Most recently she completed her Masters in Professional Writing at USC. Devo has done everything from helping writers of short films get to production to editing novels and non-fiction books for publication. Over the last five years, Devo has revisited her love of creative writing, fiction and poetry, and most recently has had material accepted in literary journals, including *Adsum, East Jasmine Review, Centrum* and a short story was honored with Koppel Award of Distinction.

STACY DEGROOT
Stacy DeGroot is a visual design and word artist living in the Arts District of downtown (DTLA) with her two young children. A native of Los Angeles with an MFA in Poetry from Antioch University, poetry is at the heart of all her artistic pursuits.

SEVEN DHAR

Seven Dhar is a poet from a bygone era. He combines East and West, Buddhist Sanskrit sensibilities, Spanish revelry, child-like shamanic mysticism, Gaelic lyricism with the playful wonderment of Lewis Carroll while remaining true to Native American roots. Educated at UCLA, Berkeley, Oxford, and Yale, Seven is the winner of the Emerging Urban Poets' 2015 SGV Poetry Festival chapbook contest, as well as the 2015 *SGV Poetry Quarterly* broadside contest, and both LA Poet Society 2015 dual National Women's Month acrostic poetry contests. He is also a LitFest Pasadena performer with Poets in Distress.

MARVIN DORSEY

At the end of a workday Marvin Dorsey travels 60 minutes by freeway, exiting on a long unpaved desert road to his ranch home in Lancaster. There he is greeted by the wind, lone tumbleweeds rambling across the sandy vista, and a variety of farmyard animals. The dichotomies of city and desert, noise and quietude, and the confines of a cage vs. the expansive freedom of the night's universe of stars, inform the heart of Marvin's poetry – where a deep interior life shares the page with the wide exterior landscape.

PAULI DUTTON

Pauli Dutton founded, coordinated, and led the Altadena Library *Poetry and Cookies Anthology* and public reading events from 2003-2014. She also wrote a poetry newsletter each year through 2013. Pauli served on this anthology's Selection Committee in 2015, 2016, and this year. She has won awards for her poems and has been published in several poetry anthologies. Recently retired after 30 years at the library, Dutton is delighted to have more time for family and friends and indulging in new writing formats. She also enjoys teaching line dancing and hosting karaoke sessions at the Altadena Senior Center.

RICHARD DUTTON

Richard Dutton retired from the fields of engineering and education with three post graduate degrees and some technical writing. Over the last ten years he has been published in several poetry anthologies including numerous editions of the *San Gabriel Valley Poetry Quarterly, Spectrum,* and Altadena Library's *Poetry and Cookies*; many publications by Poets on Site and the Southern California Haiku Group. Recent publications include the September edition of the *Bear Valley Club Newspaper* and the 2015 and 2016 editions of the *Altadena Poetry Review*. His forte is word play.

ALICIA ELKORT

Alicia Elkort edited and contributed to the chapbook *Creekside*, published under the *Berkeley Poetry Review* where she also served as an editor. Her poetry was featured in the *Ishaan Literary Review* and has been published in many others including *Elsewhere Lit, Menacing Hedge, Red Paint Hill Press, Stirring: A Literary Collection* and *Tinderbox Poetry Journal*. She was named finalist in the Two Sylvias Press Wilder Series Book Prize in 2015 and her poem *Dirt* was nominated for the 2016 Orisons Anthology. She lives in California and is currently producing a documentary on prayer when not writing poetry.

LOWAM EYASU

Because of his first and last names, the question Lowam Eyasu is usually asked is," Where are you from?" Lowam was born in Sudan, but grew up in a small country in East Africa called Eritrea. His family moved to the United States when he was two years old and he has been here ever since. Lowam first came to love text as a theatre student reading play after play in high school. He considers himself a writer because he simply loves to write and hopes you enjoy his work.

LYNN FAYNE

Lynn Fayne is a native Californian. She has a BA from UCLA, and a JD from SFVCL. She is currently retired and enjoys writing poems and painting.

EMILY FERNANDEZ

Emily Fernandez teaches composition and poetry at Pasadena City College. She lives in a little house in El Sereno with her husband, sons, chickens, and dog. She is a proud member of Las Lunas Locas, a womyn's writing group. Her poems have been published in a number of publications including *The Angel City Review, R.O.P.E.S, Edgar Allan Poet Journal, EAT/ATE, poeticdiversity, and Verse Virtual*.

MARK A. FISHER

Mark A. Fisher is a writer, poet, and playwright living in Tehachapi, CA. His poetry has appeared in: *A Sharp Piece of Awesome, Dragon Poet Review, Altadena Poetry Review, Penumbra, Elegant Rage: A Poetic Tribute to Woody Guthrie,* and many other places. His chapbook, *drifter,* is available from Amazon. His plays have appeared on California stages in Pine Mountain Club, Tehachapi, Bakersfield, and Hayward. His column "Lost in the Stars" (http://mathnerde.blogspot.com/) has appeared in Tehachapi's *The Loop* newspaper for several years. He was nominated for a Pushcart Prize in 2015. He has also won cooking ribbons at the Kern County Fair.

R. S. FORD
Robin Ford is currently studying poetry with Elline Lipkin. In the past, she was a writer/dancer in the Contemporary Ballet of Belgium and recently worked as a writer on the Belgian film pilot *Hunt* for SOIT productions. In New York City, Robin pursued a Masters in classical figure painting and worked as a production designer for indie films. She currently lives and writes in Mount Washington.

G T FOSTER
G T Foster spent his childhood in the Central San Joaquin Valley. He attended UCR and taught 25 years for LAUSD. A Vietnam era veteran, G T began his exploration into poetry in the '60s. He currently is writing his first novel, *The Butt Naked and the Been Dead* and his poetry has been published in *The Pasadena Weekly, San Gabriel Valley Quarterly, Spectrum,* and *Altadena Poetry Review 2016.* He was nominated for a Pushcart Prize in 2016.

ELSA FRAUSTO
Elsa Frausto is a bilingual poet from Buenos Aires, Argentina. She has read widely in California, Mexico, and Oregon, and her work has appeared in diverse publications, among them *La Porte des Poètes, la-luciérnaga.com, Spineflower Blues, Chuparosa Calendars, South of You, Spectrum* and the *Altadena Poetry Review* 2016. Currently, she is Poet Laureate of Sunland-Tujunga (2014-2017) where she has lived with her family for close to thirty years. She coordinates and hosts the monthly Wide Open Readings.

MARTINA ROBLES GALLEGOS
Martina comes from Mexico and lived in Altadena and Pasadena through high school. She then moved to Oxnard and attended community college, and then California State University, Northridge and got her teaching credential. She taught for almost 18 years in Hueneme Elementary School District. Works have appeared in *Altadena Review, Hometown Pasadena, Basta!, Spectrum, Latino Authors,* and *Silver Birch Press.* http://poetry309.wordpress.com. She was named as a "Top 10 San Gabriel Valley Poet 2016" by Spectrum Publications

DAMIAN GONZALEZ
Damian Gonzalez is a New York born, Los Angeles cultivated writer, artist, and award-winning filmmaker. He co-produced *Poetry Palooza* (2013), a Southern California non-profit touring open mic and his short films garnered the attention of the *Creative Artist Agency*, which sponsored him to attend both the *Sundance Film Festival* and the 2012 *Karlovy Film Festival* near Prague as an "Emerging Talent."

CHARLES HARMON
Charles Harmon first published a story in the local newspaper in fourth grade. He has produced hundreds of poems, songs, stories, articles, photographs, artwork, screenplays and assembled collected poems, and is trying to get two books published. He won a NSTA national science teaching award and $10,000 in 2001 for his project, "Don't Be a Crash Test Dummy!" He has used poetry and songs to motivate students, challenging them to write their own. He reviewed, edited, contributed to five textbooks for Houghton Mifflin. A world traveler, Charles spent five years overseas and has taught English, composition as well as sciences. He was named a "Top 10 San Gabriel Valley Poet 2016" by Spectrum Publications.

HAZEL CLAYTON HARRISON
Hazel Clayton Harrison earned her B.S. and M.ED from Kent State University. Her poetry has been published in many anthologies, including the *Altadena Poetry Review: Anthology 2016* and *Coiled Serpent*. Her memoir, *Crossing the River Ohio*, is available on Amazon.

DAVID HUMPREYS
Dave Humphreys began his career in marketing and television promotions, where his interest in short form story telling has always been a bonus. He has sold a screenplay to ABC Family (AKA FreeForm), written for *Toyfare* magazine, and co-created the *B-Movie Podcast Review*, Cinema Craptaculus.

ARMINE IKNADOSSIAN
In 2015, Armine Iknadossian retired from teaching in order to support the literary arts and to focus on her two manuscripts *god(l)ess: the L is silent* and *Resident Alien*. She is currently one of the bookstore managers at Beyond Baroque Bookstore aka The Scott Wannberg Poetry Lounge where you can purchase her newly released chapbook *United States of Love & Other Poems*. She is looking forward to serving as a Writer in the Schools (WITS) for Red Hen Press beginning in the fall of 2017. Please

visit www.armineiknadossian.com to view her previously published work.

GEDDA ILVES
Gedda was born in Harbin, North China to Russian parents. She lived in Shanghai during WWII and came to Los Angeles in 1951. Her first book of poems, *grains of life* was published in 2005; *a view from within* was published in 2008 and *interval* in 2011. In 2006 she received the Editor's Award for Outstanding Achievement in Poetry from Poetry.com and the International Library of Poetry. Her poems have appeared in several literary journals and three anthologies. She is the recipient of awards from the London Book Festival, the Los Angeles Book Festival, and was a finalist in The Eric Hoffer Awards for 2012. Her fourth book of poems, *at the threshold* is a runner up for the Paris Book Festival Award in 2015.

GERDA GOVINE ITUARTE
Gerda Govine Ituarte, Ed.D. is author of *Future Awakes in Mouth of NOW*, (2016), *Alterations| Thread Light Through Eye of Storm* (2015) and *Oh, Where is My Candle Hat?* (2012). Her work appeared in *Coiled Serpent, Indefinite Space, Journal of Modern Poetry, San Gabriel Valley Poetry Quarterly, Spectrum, The Altadena Poetry Review: Anthology* 2015-2016 and *Frontera Esquina Magazine* in Tijuana. *Online Dryland Los Angeles Arts and Letters, Hometown Pasadena* and *Ms. Aligned*. Her readings include: Avenue 50 Studio, Book Show Bookstore, Lit Crawl L.A., 2012-2015, Tia Chucha Cultural Center, The Coffee Gallery, The Last Bookstore, and The World Stage. Gerda was named a "Top 10 San Gabriel Valley Poet 2016" by Spectrum Publications. www.poetryartbookstation.com

LISA'ANNE G. IVEY
Lisa'Anne Ivey is a proud Jamaican-born-and-raised, LA-based actor, model and writer. She is currently taking a year off from her former two careers to travel and complete the script of her very first feature film which she hopes to start filming in the fall of 2017. She hopes to finish a series of children's story books written with a poetic flair and filled with anecdotes from her six magical years as a nanny and an aunty! Blogs about her wanderlusting weekends and her life's personal and artistic journey can be found with by searching "#goldenhitchhiker" and her poetry with "#IveyPoetry."

KATHLEEN JACOBSON

Kathleen Jacobson has been writing poetry all her life and she weaves her deepest feelings into poems. For her, it is healing and creative at the same time. Ms. Jacobson has published poems in various poetry journals and blogs at the Huffington Post. She works in the medical field but lives in the arts. Ms. Jacobson is a student of Japanese tea ceremony and an amateur artist, dancer and flutist. Visit her website and learn more about her at http://www.huffingtonpost.com/author/kathleen-jacobson

BRIONY JAMES

Briony James has been nearly a decade in Altadena, experiencing and tasting the mountain air. Her world is sage-scented and full of chaos. She has served on the *Altadena Poetry Review* Selection Committee during 2015, 2016, and 2017.

JEFFRY JENSEN

Jeffry Jensen resides in Pasadena, but his work takes him throughout the Los Angeles area. He is the Adult Librarian at the Granada Hills Branch of the Los Angeles Public Library, an adjunct librarian at Glendale Community College, and an adjunct professor at Los Angeles Valley College. Jeffry was named one of the Top 10 Poets in the San Gabriel Valley by Spectrum 2016. He is also the author of several poetry chapbooks and his artwork has been included in a number of shows.

PATRICK JIMENEZ

Patrick Jimenez is a poet as well as a Hip Hop artist who goes by the name S.A.G.A. Emcee. He resides in Alhambra, CA, and his purpose is to continue moving music and poetry forward with passion. We all have a story but not everyone has a voice. Patrick hopes to be that voice and to express his views as well as the views of the newer generation.

LOIS P. JONES

Lois P. Jones has work published or forthcoming in *Poemeleon* and several anthologies including: *The Poet's Quest for God* (Eyewear Publishing), *Wide Awake: Poetry of Los Angeles and Beyond (The Pacific Coast Poetry Series), 30 Days (Tupelo Press)* and *Good-Bye Mexico* (Texas Review Press). Publications include *Narrative*, American Poetry Journal, *One* (Jacar Press), *the Tupelo Quarterly*, *The Warwick Review, Tiferet, Cider Press Review* and other journals in the U.S. and abroad. Lois's poems have won honors under judges Kwame Dawes, Ruth Ellen Kocher and others. She is the winner of the 2012 Tiferet Poetry Prize and the 2012 Liakoura Prize and a five-time Pushcart nominee. She was recently shortlisted for the Bridport Prize in poetry (2016). Lois is Poetry Editor of *Kyoto Journal*, host of KPFK's *Poets Café* and co-host of Moonday Poetry.

LORELEI KAY
Lorelei Kay published an award-winning memoir, *From Mormon to Mermaid*, in spring 2016. She also writes poetry which has appeared in anthologies and magazines. She attended Brigham Young University on a journalism scholarship. She is presently working on a poetry collection as well as a new novel.

LALO KIKIRIKI
lalo kikiriki was born in Oklahoma, but grew up in Texas and moved to California in 1979. After ten years as morning show host on Pacifica Radio Houston and publication of a chapbook, *Old Old Movies, Other Visions,* (with Pam Palmer), lalo earned a Master's Degree in Humanities from Cal State Dominguez Hills in 2007 and is a ZZyZx Writer, itinerant accordionist, and queen of Poetrypalooza 2015.

MINA KIRBY
Mina Kirby, retired mathematics professor, enjoys writing both prose and poetry. Her newest books are *Threads of My Life ~ An Illustrated Collection of Poems* and *Lilacs and Home-Grown Tomatoes ~ How It Was Back Then*. Mina has been a featured poet at a number of venues in Southern California and Maryland. She lives in Altadena with her family, her fur kids, and many spiders.

CYBELE GARCIA KOHEL
Cybele Garcia Kohel is a poet and arts administrator living and working in Pasadena, California. She has been writing poetry since her teens. Born in Puerto Rico, Ms. Kohel writes about life through the many lenses provided by her diverse background, her Generation X upbringing, and the streets of Los Angeles. While her journal and pencil await her at the desk, she is busy supporting arts education and young artists in their artistic quests.

DEBORAH P KOLODJI
Deborah P Kolodji is the California regional coordinator for the Haiku Society of America, moderator of the Southern California Haiku Study Group, and past president of the Science Fiction Poetry Association. With more than 900 haiku in publications such as *Frogpond, Modern Haiku,* the *Heron's Nest, Bottle,* and *Mayfly*, her first full length book of

haiku, *highway of sleeping towns*, was recently published by Shabda Press and is available on Amazon.

LINDA KRAAI
Linda Kraai is a retired classroom teacher of orthopedically handicapped children and was also a mentor teacher. She is enrolled in a poetry class in the Osha Lifelong Learning Institute at California State University, Fullerton, and attends a weekly poetry workshop in Claremont, California. Linda enjoys piano (accompanying a violinist), bridge, reading, opera, and concerts. She volunteers providing assistance for youth in foster care and raising funds for scholarships for women.

KITTY KROGER
Kitty Kroger, a Pasadena resident, began writing poetry in July of this year. She has been published in *Spectrums 6 and 7*. Before retirement, she was a high school E.S.L. teacher in Los Angeles. She is also an enthusiastic piano player, has written a novel called *Dancing with Mao and Miguel,* and edits a blog on "Voices of the Sixties and Seventies." Currently she's writing a memoir about the difficulties of raising a son as a single mother. But she always makes time for poetry.

SHARON KUNDE
Sharon Kunde grew up in a small town in northern Illinois. Since then, she has lived, taught, and studied in Boston, Albania, Mongolia, New York City, and Los Angeles. She is currently a PhD candidate in English at the University of California, Irvine. Her dissertation, for which she was recently awarded an ACLS/Mellon Dissertation Completion Fellowship, proposes a post humanist reframing of the traditional American Transcendentalist canon. Her stories and poems have appeared or are forthcoming in *Spoon River Poetry Review*, *Midwestern Gothic*, *Hotel Amerika*, *Foothill*, *cold-drill*, and others. Her thoughts on hiking, relationality, embodiment, and the more-than-human can be found on her blog, *Throughhike: Down in the Dirt of the California Backcountry* (throughhike.wordpress.com). She lives in Altadena, California with her husband and two sons.

LEAH LAGMAY
Leah Lagmay, born in Los Angeles, raised in New York and New Jersey, now a longtime resident of Southern California, resides in Arcadia. She is retired from the fashion industry where she worked as an assistant to several designers. She has attended Otis Art Institute, University of Maine and Pasadena City College. Leah has always enjoyed drawing, painting

and many other creative arts, one of which is writing. She attends a poetry group at CSC in Pasadena.

KATHY LEONARD
Kathy Leonard wrote her first poem at age 7, already a lover of words, of books, of songs. She was nicknamed *Webster* in school, held her head high and kept writing. Now she is a Middle-School English teacher, and a poet who attends Raven's Poetry Group in Claremont and Valley Poets in Glendora. She appreciates and cherishes her tribe of poet colleagues who encourage her to publish, and most importantly, to honor her sacred voice with her words on the page.

NANCY LIND
A recent transplant from New York, Nancy Lind is a retired professor of English literature. She has studied poetry in workshops with award-winning poet Dan Masterson. Nancy has been a founder and leader of two Dickens Fellowship branches. She currently resides in Pasadena and has been active in regional poetry events. Most recently, she has been published in *Impulse, the Journal of Modern Poetry, Ibis Head,* and the *Altadena Poetry Review* 2015 and 2016. She is a 2015 Pushcart Prize nominee.

JANIS ALBRIGHT LUKSTEIN
Janis Albright Lukstein loves the sound of playful, rhyming poetry and welcomes you to the *Bear Valley CUB Newspaper's Poetry Corner,* published by Faith at bvcub.att.net. Janis saves the third Saturday from 2-4pm for the Pasadena SoCaHaikuStudyGroup. Poets-on-Site meets at CalTech and read/perform poetry and later publish tanka in *Ribbons.* Other publications include *Mariposa* of Haiku Poets and *Members Anthologies of the Palos Verdes Library,* Yuki Teikei Haiku Society, Haiku Society of America and the *International Poems of the World.* Join Janis' interactive sing-a-longs at the annual January Palos Verdes Peninsula Horsemen's Cowboy Poetry and Music Festival.

RICK LUPERT
Los Angeles poet Rick Lupert created the Poetry Super Highway (http://poetrysuperhighway.com) and hosted the Cobalt Cafe weekly reading for almost 21 years. He's authored 20 collections of poetry, most recently *Making Love to the 50 Ft. Woman* and edited the anthologies *Ekphrastia Gone Wild, A Poet's Haggadah,* and *The Night Goes on All Night.* He writes the Jewish Poetry Blog From the Lupertverse for www.Jewish.Journal.com and the daily web comic *Cat and Banana* with

fellow Los Angeles poet Brendan Constantine. He's widely published and reads his poetry wherever they let him.

JOE LUSNIA
Joe Lusnia is a husband, father, worker, writer, living in Pasadena with his wife Cindy and their three sons. Joe enjoys taking literature and writing courses at PCC.

RADOMIR VOJTECH LUZA
Radomir Vojtech Luza is Poet Laureate of North Hollywood, CA. He is a Pushcart Prize Nominee and author of 30 books. His poetry has been published in over 80 anthologies, literary journals, websites, blogs, newspapers, magazines and other media. Radomir is also a union actor, theatre critic, stand-up comedian and host/curator of readings across the country. He edits and publishes the literary magazine, "Voices in the Library" through Red Doubloon Publishing, the publishing arm of Radman Productions.

KARINEH MAHDESSIAN
Karineh Mahdessian, a community social worker, is interested in people and art. She hosts the La Palabra reading series at Avenue 50 Studios and co-founded and co-facilitates Las Lunas Locas. She loves tacos, earrings, books, and basketball. She was nominated for a Pushcart Prize in 2016.

SHAHÉ MANKERIAN
Shahé Mankerian's most recent manuscript, *History of Forgetfulness*, was a finalist at four prestigious competitions: the 2013 Crab Orchard Series in Poetry Open Competition, the 2013 Bibby First Book Competition, the Quercus Review Press, Fall Poetry Book Award 2013, and the 2014 White Pine Press Poetry Prize. His poems have been published in numerous literary magazines. He was nominated for a Pushcart Prize in 2015.

MIRA N. MATARIC, Ph.D.
Dr. Mira N. Mataric has had 42 books published bilingually (poetry, prose and translations), with thousands of citations in other publications internationally. Recipient of over 20 international awards, she has four Presidential medals for volunteer work in education. She has taught World Literature, Creative Writing, Special Education and Foreign Languages to youth and seniors for many years. She edited a literary magazine for 20 years, founded and chaired Women in the Arts, Inc. She is active as a public speaker, facilitator of workshops and public poetry

readings. Translated into several languages, her work is included in numerous anthologies on four continents.

PAT MURPHY MCCLELLAND
Pat Murphy McClelland taught "Writing for Healing" at the UC/SF Comprehensive Cancer Center. She has a memoir about Flo Kennedy (forthcoming in the anthology *Mentors that Matter,* due out in December from *Stories of You*). Her poetry appears in various publications, such as *blynkt* (forthcoming); *Chronicles of Eve* (Paper Swans Press, 2016); *Caravel Literary Journal*; *Snapdragon Journal;* *ARAS Connections: Image and Archetype*; the *Altadena Poetry Review; Feile-Festa Literary Journal*; *Atlas Poetica*; and a chapbook, *Turnings*. She is endlessly revising a memoir, "The Masks of Grief," hoping to eventually reach a receptive audience.

ALICE MEERSON
Born and raised in Chicago, Alice received a BA from the University of Illinois at Chicago with a major in history. She lived overseas for several years before settling in the Altadena/Pasadena area, where she earned an MA from Pacific Oaks College in Human Development. She taught Special Education for many years in Glendale, CA prior to formally retiring. She continues to teach, take classes, write, and travel.

NANCY MORLEY
Nancy is a Jersey girl—that doesn't mean big hair and gum popping—it means attitude and a love of what Jersey offers—four seasons, great pizza and the City. So what is she doing in endless summer? His name is Nicholas, and he is four. He calls her husband Papa and calls Nancy Yamma—and is the joy of their lives. And he lives in Pasadena. So, she packed 67 boxes, crated Harry James the beagle and moved here. Pasadena offers a gift—mobility. Nancy is legally blind, but the city is walkable and transportation accessible to museums, libraries, and bookstores. Nirvana to a retired English teacher/librarian.

NANCY MURPHY
Nancy Murphy's poems have appeared in *The South Carolina Review, Baltimore Review, Eclipse, Thirteenth Moon* and *The Louisville Review*. She also writes personal stories and has performed in Los Angeles series including *Tasty Words, Expressing Motherhood, Max10, WordNow,* and *Muse Literary Salon.* In June, she performed a one-woman show about turning 60 called "Freak Out" as part of the Hollywood Fringe Festival where it won an Encore Producers Award. Nancy has a B.A.degree in

American Studies from Union College in Schenectady, NY, and has studied writing at UCLA Extension Writers' Program, Beyond Baroque in Venice, and with various private teachers and workshops.

ELLIOT NEGRIN
Elliot Negrin is a transgender fourteen-year-old poet who loves writing, reading, drawing, and music. Elliot has been writing poetry seriously since he was about twelve years old when his English teacher taught poetry for a month. He fell in love with the art form and has been working on his skills ever since. A lot of his poetry stems from the adversary he's faced from lack of acceptance from those around him, and occasionally himself. Being a wordsmith is his greatest passion, and he hopes that by getting an early head start he will be able to succeed in the adult world.

JANET NIPPELL
Janet Nippell was born and grew up in Los Angeles and now lives in Pasadena. She's had poems in *Rattle*, *A Narrow Fellow*, *Christianity & Literature*, the *Altadena Poetry Review*, as well as Tia Chucha's *Coiled Serpent* anthology. With Ben Yandell, she wrote *Mostly on Foot—A Year in L.A.* (Floating Island, 1989), narrating walks in two voices.

TOTI O'BRIEN
Toti O'Brien's poetry has appeared in *Extract(s)*, *Gyroscope*, *The Lightning Key*, and *Surreal Poetics*, among other journals and anthologies.

MARSHA OSEAS
After spending the better part of four decades working in law firms and later for the government where the writing offended her with its purposeful verbosity and incomprehensibility, Marsha is relieved to be writing for herself.

ALICE PERO
Alice Pero's poetry has been published in many magazines and anthologies including *Nimrod*, *National Poetry Review*, *Poet Lore*, *Coiled Serpent*, *Wide Awake* and many others. Her book, *Thawed Stars,* was praised by Kenneth Koch as having "clarity and surprises." Pero is also the founder of "Moonday," a reading series which has been ongoing in the Los Angeles area since 2002. An accomplished concert flutist, she created the Windsong Players Chamber Ensemble in 2015. Pero has created dialogue poems with over 20 poets internationally and was a Pushcart

Prize nominee in 2016. She continues to do poetry features around the Southland and the East Coast while performing with Windsong.

DALTON PERRY (dp)
Dalton is a native of Southern California. He has written sporadically for about 50 years. His writings have appeared in many diverse publications.

ALBIE PRECIADO
Albie Preciado was born into a family of reminiscers; narratives are in his DNA. He spends his days listening to and telling stories in a corporate capacity but finds poetry allows him to give voice to a part of himself that might otherwise never see the light of day. Aside from his passion for words, Albie has an unshakable thirst for knowledge and has amassed a quiver full of interests. Preferring the autodidactic approach, he has dabbled in blacksmithing, woodworking, and taxidermy. He is motivated by a desire to pursue anything he has ever romanticized.

THELMA T. REYNA, Ph.D.
Thelma T. Reyna's books have collectively won 8 national literary awards. She has written 4 books: a short story collection (*The Heavens Weep for Us* and *Other Stories)*, 2 poetry chapbooks (*Breath & Bone* and *Hearts in Common);* and a full-length poetry collection, *Rising, Falling, All of Us.* Her fiction, poetry, and nonfiction have appeared in literary journals, anthologies, textbooks, blogs, and regional media for over 25 years. As Poet Laureate in Altadena, 2014-2016, she edited the *Altadena Poetry Review: Anthology 2015*, as well as the 2016 anthology, which was the Winner of the 2016 Book Excellence Award and the Beverly Hills Book Award (Anthology categories). She was selected as a "Top 10 San Gabriel Valley Poet: 2016" by Spectrum Publications.

R. S. ROCHA
R. S. Rocha is a native of Los Angeles and a published author. His family has lived in The City of the Angels for six generations. He currently resides in the Highland Park neighborhood of Los Angeles and is active in the community's visual and literary arts.

SUSAN ROGERS
Susan Rogers considers poetry a vehicle for light and positive energy. She is a practitioner of Sukyo Mahikari—a spiritual practice promoting positive thoughts, words and action. www.sukyomahikari.org Her poems are included in numerous anthologies and journals including *The Best*

Poems of San Diego, Pirene's Fountain and *Saint Julian's Press*. She was nominated for a Pushcart Prize and interviewed by Lois P. Jones for KPFK's *Poet's Café*.

DIANA ROSEN
Diana Rosen provides content websites on food and beverage, has written 10 nonfiction books and co-authored three others; published more than 40 pieces of flash fiction, poetry, and essays in print and online media including *Rattle*, www.silverbirch.com, www.verse-virtual.com, and in several anthologies.

CATHIE SANDSTROM
Cathie Sandstrom's poems have appeared in *Ploughshares, The Southern Review, Lyric, Comstock Review,* and *Cider Press Review* among others, and is forthcoming in *The Southern*. She is published in the anthology *Wide Awake: Poets of Los Angeles and Beyond*. A poem with essay appears in *Master Class: The Poetry Mystique.* Her manuscript *All the Land Around Us* was a finalist for Perugia Press. A finalist in the Poets & Writers' California Writers Exchange, her poem "You, Again" is in the artists' book collection at the Getty Museum in Los Angeles. A military brat, she finally stopped wandering to settle in Sierra Madre, California.

ELSA M. J. SEIFERT
Elsa M. J. Seifert, M.A., is an Interfaith Spiritual Director and a long-time resident of Altadena. After raising three sons, managing a business and editing a Southern California newspaper, she now spends much of her time volunteering for non-profits and writing essays, short stories, and poetry. Her poems and prose have appeared in these anthologies: *Altadena Poetry Review* 2015 and 2016, *The Courage to Write* (Falcon Creek 2011), *Authors in Our Midst* ebook 2013, and *Poetry and Cookies*, 2011–2014. Her prose has appeared in the *Southern California Nevada News* 1998-2008 (an insert of the nation United Church of Christ News), and she has published a chapbook of poems, *The Source* 2014.

NANCY SHIFFRIN
The poem in this book is from *The Vast Unknowing* (Infinity Publishing, B&N.com). Nancy is also the author of the poetry book *Game with Variations* (unibook.com). Her novel, *Out of the Garden,* is available at Lulu.com, along with an essay, *Invoking Anais Nin.* Her work appears in *Lummox Journal, Philosopher Stone, San Diego Poetry Annual,* and has appeared in the *Altadena Poetry Review.*

JULIA ROBINSON SHIMIZU

Julia Robinson Shimizu is a writer whose day job is writing. She has focused her career on providing a voice to disadvantaged communities. She serves non-profit organizations in the Los Angeles Metropolitan area and is the author of two books. Her work has appeared in literary journals including *The Sun* and has been published in the *Los Angeles Times*. She occasionally shares her poetry via twitter at *@JuliaThinksThis*.

DOROTHY SKILES

Dorothy Skiles served as Poet Laureate of Sunland-Tujunga from 2012 to 2014 and is President of the Village Poets of Sunland-Tujunga who sponsor monthly poetry readings. She also facilitates a monthly poetry group at the Verdugo Hills YMCA. Her chapbooks include: *The Sidewalk Gallery (1979), Ear to Earth* (1996), *Spine Flower Blues* (1999)—a collaborative work by the Chuparosa Writers—*Riddle in the Rain* (2003)—a collaborative work with Marlene Hitt. Her poems have appeared in *Meditation on Divine Names*, Moonrise Press 2012, and *From Benicia With Love*, Accent Digital Publishing, Redding CA 2013. In July 2015, she was featured in *Colorado Boulevard.net in Pasadena, Mapping the Artist—Dorothy Skiles*. In April 20016, her poems appeared in the *Altadena Poetry Review: Anthology, 2016*.

BECKY SKOGLUND

Becky Skoglund is a native of Long Beach, California, and a fairly new resident of Altadena, happily trading the ocean for the mountains. She has a B.A. in both English Literature and Creative Writing from CSULB and an M.A. in Spiritual Psychology from the University of Santa Monica. She's an intuitive with a passion for transforming people, places and things and enjoys spending time with her partner and their furry, four-legged family. She's an artist at heart and often spends time in the creative world, writing for personal enjoyment, intuitively cooking, and singing to herself.

DAVID SLAVIN

David Slavin was born and raised in a small Midwestern town just north of Los Angeles. You may know it as Glendale. He was a host of the LMU Extension Program Reading Series, has been active in Beyond Baroque workshops, and has studied under some of Los Angeles' finest poets. His work has been published in *Askew, Quill & Parchment,* and published as Lithuanian translations in *Literatura & Menas*.

JANET STERNBURG
Janet Sternburg is the author of two books of creative nonfiction, *Phantom Limb* (University of Nebraska Press, American Lives series) and *White Matter* (Hawthorne Books), as well as a book of poetry, *Optic Nerve: Photopoems* (Red Hen Press) and the iconic two volumes, *The Writer on Her Work* (W.W. Norton). A monograph of her fine-art photography, *Overspilling World* (Distanz Verlag,) has recently been published, with a foreword by Wim Wenders.

ROBERT STEWART
Robert Stewart is 76 and a retired, printing stripper. He holds a BFA from the University of New Mexico and did graduate studies at LATTC (color separation). He has lived in Los Angles for fifty years, mainly in Echo Park and Silverlake. His themes in poetry are autobiographical, LA scenes, and contemporary life as it exists. He is a regular at Red Door Poetry.

CALOKIE (aka CARL STILWELL)
CaLokie is a retired teacher who taught for over 30 years mostly in the Los Angeles Unified School District. He was born during the depression in Oklahoma and came to California in 1959 and has lived here ever since. He has lived in Pasadena since 2003. He has had poems published in *Blue Collar Review, Canary, Life and Legends, Lummox, Pearl, Prism, Revolutionary Poets Brigade—Los Angeles, Spectrum, Struggle and Verse-Virtual*. He also has had poems included in the anthologies, *An Eye for an Eye Makes the Whole World Blind/Poets on 911* and *In the Arms of Words: Poems for Tsunami Relief*. He was selected as a "Top 10 San Gabriel Valley Poet: 2016" by Spectrum Publications.

SACHI TERRY
Sachi is an Altadena native studying English and Modern Languages. Her latest work was featured in a 2011 edition of *Inscape* and the literary magazines *decomP*. She spends her time working as a server in a retirement home, learning about health (bearing daily shots of wheatgrass and ginger), and participating in artistic projects with students and local photographers.

JUDITH TERZI
Judith Terzi's poetry has appeared or is forthcoming in journals such as *Atlanta Review* (International Publication Prize, 2015), *Caesura, Raintown Review, Spillway, Unsplendid* and in anthologies such as *Malala: Poems for Malala Yoursafzai and Wide Awake: The Poets of Los*

Angeles and Beyond. Her poem, "Apple Pie" was shortlisted for the 2016 Able Muse Write Prize. *If You Spot Your Brother Floating By* is her latest chapbook from Kattywompus Pres. Her poetry has been nominated for Best of the Net and Web.

MARY LANGER THOMPSON

Mary Langer Thompson's poems, short stories, and essays appear in various journals and anthologies. She is a contributor to two poetry writing texts, *The Working Poet* (Autumn Press, 2009) and *Women and Poetry: Writing, Revising, Publishing and Teaching* (McFarland, 2012), and was the 2012 Senior Poet Laureate of California. A retired school principal and former secondary English teacher, Langer Thompson received her Ed.D. from the University of California, Los Angeles. She enjoys conducting poetry workshops for schools, prisons, and in her community of the high desert.

MAJA TROCHIMCZYK, Ph.D.

Maja Trochimczyk is a Polish American poet, music historian, photographer, and author of six books on music. Her most recent book is *Frédéric Chopin: A Research and Information Guide* (rev. ed., 2015). Trochimczyk's seven books of poetry include *Rose Always, Miriam's Iris, Slicing the Bread, Into Light, The Rainy Bread,* and two anthologies, *Chopin with Cherries* and *Meditations on Divine Names.* A former Poet Laureate of Sunland-Tujunga, she is the founder of Moonrise Press, and Board Secretary of the Polish American Historical Association. Hundreds of her poems, studies, articles and chapters have appeared in English and in translations. She is a recipient of awards from the American Council of Learned Societies, Polish Ministry of Culture, Polish American Historical Association, McGill University, and USC. www.trochimczyk.net.

CLAUDINE VOZNICK

Claudine Voznick is an Executive Assistant at the University of Southern California. Her degree is in Liberal Studies with a concentration in Literature from Mt. St. Mary's College. Her love of poetry started in high school with a fascination for the English poets, Alfred Lord Tennyson, T.S. Eliot and Elizabeth Barrett Browning. While these poets still and will always hold a special place in her heart, she has become more aware, appreciative of "our own," such as Frank O'Hara, Ann Sexton and Mary Oliver. Poetry is the answer to most of the unrequited questions of her heart.

LORI WALL-HOLLOWAY

A wife, mother and proud grandmother of nine grandchildren, Wall-Holloway lives in the San Gabriel Valley where her poetry has appeared in a number of publications. Some of these include the *San Gabriel Valley Poetry Quarterly,* several of the *Poetry and Cookies* anthologies, the 2015 and 2016 *Altadena Poetry Review* as well as in the *Spectrum* anthologies.

JENNIFER WELSH

Jennifer earned her B.A. from Purdue University and her M.A. from Loyola Marymount University. Her poetry, creative non-fiction, and a collection review have been published in *L.A. Miscellany*, *The Truth About the Fact*, and *Poetry International Magazine.* She has been a panelist at the West Hollywood Book Fair and a presenter at the 2011 PAMLA Scripps Conference. She was the Producing Director of the Black Dahlia Theatre, called "A Living Treasure" by *L.A. Weekly* and "Best Small Theatre" by *Los Angeles Magazine.* Her industry credits include work for CBS, ABC, FOX, MTV, MGM, Oxygen, Lifetime, and Paramount Pictures/MTV Films.

MARI WERNER

Mari Werner's work has been published in *Rattle, Altadena Poetry Review 2016, Poetry Quarterly, Colorado Boulevard,* and elsewhere. She is a regular reader at poetry readings in the greater Los Angeles area and has featured at the Rattle Reading Series, Village Poets, and Second Sunday. She was a resident of Altadena for four years, and now lives in Claremont, California.

KATH ABELA WILSON

Kath Abela Wilson is creator and leader of Poets on Site, an ever-expanding group inspired by art, music, science and nature, performing on the sites of their inspiration. She travels the world with her mathematician-flute player husband Rick. She hosts three workshops a week, as well as themed salon events at Caltech, their home in Pasadena, and at the Storrier Stearns Garden. Her pen name honors her mother's (1920-2015) maiden name, Abela. She is secretary of the Tanka Society of America.

JOHN L. WILTSHIRE

John's parents, Mary and Roy Wiltshire, adopted him and raised him with love and a strong sense of right and wrong. He believes a man's worth is not measured by the quality of his achievements but rather by the compassion in his heart. He has been an artist all of his life: acting, dancing, painting, and now writing poetry and a bit of prose. He is grateful to Julie Arthur for her editing and general support, and to his friend Brian Thorpe who encouraged him to write more. He is learning to do just that.

JOE WITT

Joe Witt resides in Altadena, with his wife, Roz, and their two cats, ShadieLadie and Mouse. They have one son, two grandsons and two step-grandchildren, who keep them busy. Retired from JPL in 2002, Joe is currently learning to kiteboard. He is in Mira Mataric's creative writing class at the Pasadena Sr. Center and has had a tanka, a haiku, and a poem published.

ROZ WITT

Roz Witt resides in Altadena, CA, with her husband Joe, and their two cats, ShadieLadie and Mouse. They have one son, two grandsons and two step grandchildren, who keep them busy. She loves to garden, takes Tai Chi and dances with the Pasadena Folk Dance Coop.

J.K. WON

J.K. Won has lived in Southern California most of his life and writes mainly short form poetry. He participates in poetry readings in the local area, and his short form poetry has been published in a few journals.

ANNETTE WONG

Annette is a poet and a lawyer living in Los Angeles.

HELEN YAGAKE

Last year for the first time since high school (a million years ago), Helen had a poem published in the *Altadena Poetry Review* and gave her first reading. She now calls herself a poet.

SHARON YOFAN

Sharon Yofan began writing lyrics to original songs as a high school student in the '50s. For the past twenty years, she has been writing personal poetry as a form of journaling. She lives in Studio City, California.

www.ingramcontent.com/pod-product-compliance
Lightning Source LLC
LaVergne TN
LVHW011220080426
835509LV00005B/241